CONTENTS

Blue-livered GWR 4-6-0 No. 6023 *King Edward II* heads away from Loughborough Central on January 26, 2013, during the winter steam gala. ROBIN JONES

WELCOME
to the Greater Great Central!

Visiting GWR 2-8-0 No. 3803 approaches Quorn & Woodhouse on January 26, 2014, during the winter steam gala. ALAN CORFIELD

Mention the Great Central Railway today and images of the magnificent heritage line between Loughborough and Leicester North immediately spring to mind.

It is the world's only double track heritage trunk railway, and in the four decades since the section was revived as a heritage line, a tourist attraction and educational resource, a sizeable chunk of Britain's preserved steam fleet has graced its metals.

LNER A3 Pacific No. 4472 *Flying Scotsman*, the world's most famous steam locomotive, postwar record holder LNER A4 No. 60007 *Sir Nigel Gresley* and new-build Peppercorn A1 Pacific No. 60163 *Tornado* are just a few of the illustrious names that have been rostered on the line.

However, the Loughborough operation is only part of the great heritage of the original Great Central Railway and its London Extension from Annesley to Marylebone, the last trunk route to be built in Britain before the High Speed 1 Channel Tunnel Rail Link, which had formed part of its promoter Edward Watkin's unrealised ambition for trains to run beneath the English Channel in late Victorian times.

The London Extension was a 'Johnny come lately' railway, opening at the tail end of the Victorian age, when the great main lines that make up our national network today had been opened for decades. Already there were three other trunk routes linking London to the north, and only one town on the London Extension, Lutterwoth, was not already served by rail.

However, it had several advantages over its rivals, not least of all the lack of sharp gradients and level crossings which permitted its Manchester to London expresses to run at very high speeds. The Great Central's state-of-the-art dining trains became a byword for comfort and luxury.

However, in terms of patronage, it always trailed behind its longer-established rivals, and freight was a primary source of income.

Doubling up on existing routes, it became a prime target for Dr Beeching, and the London Extension was dismembered and closed in the mid- to late-Sixties. This was before it fully dawned on everyone that it would have, as Watkin envisaged, made an unrivalled route taking both freight and passengers from the Midlands and north to Paris and beyond today had it been allowed to survive for a few more years. The London Extension was the biggest Beeching closure and one of the most regrettable.

Revivalists were on the scene at Loughborough around the same time that the final passenger services ran into Nottingham's makeshift Arkwright Street terminus in 1969, and slowly but surely they pieced together the splendid heritage line we enjoy today.

Two decades later, volunteers looked at the section which survived between Loughborough and the outskirts of Nottingham, and so began the rise of the Great Central Railway (Nottingham), which unlike its southern counterpart not only has a main line connection but carries real freight too.

The two Great Central railways of today, however, were not the first heritage presence on the London Extension. That honour goes to the Buckinghamshire Railway Centre, based since the Sixties on an expansive site at Quainton Road station, through which Great Central expresses once thundered to and from the capital.

Newly green-liveried BR Standard 9F 2-10-0 No. 92214, the latest addition to the Great Central Railway steam fleet, departs from Loughborough Central on June 22, 2014. ALAN WEAVER

Left: Great Central Railway 8B 4-4-2 No. 264, built to a John Robinson design in July 1904 by Beyer Peacock. It was renumbered by the LNER as No. 5264 and then in 1946 as No. 2903, which it carried until it was withdrawn from 40A Lincoln shed in June 1949. It would had been given the British Railways running number 62903 had it survived in traffic. ROBIN JONES COLLECTION

In this volume, we look at these and other parts of the Great Central empire that are thankfully still with us.

In Britain, only two locomotives, and a handful of unrestored coaches, have survived from the original line, and are both in the National Collection (although there are three more in Australia and just maybe, at some time, one or more might be brought home).

Sad, but still, no matter. Today's two Loughborough outfits each provide a stupendous stage whereby trains from any company or region can be successfully re-created on an authentic main line setting so

wondrously typical of the Changeover Years, the last decade of steam and the first of diesels. Located near the heart of England, and well survived by both motorway links and rail, the name Great Central takes on a double meaning.

We also look at the much-loved Dinting Railway Centre which was set up on part of the GCR, and which was a welcome bolthole for steam in a decade where so many locomotives went to the scrapyard.

Then there is the field of electric stock. Thankfully, several vehicles from the GCR's Grimsby & Immingham Tramway survive, as do a handful of locomotives from another line

which promised so much but was closed early, many think before its time, the Woodhead Route across the Pennines.

Also part of the original GCR portfolio was the South Yorkshire Railway, and it too is represented in preservation, in the form of the Elsecar Heritage Railway near Barnsley.

The Loughborough-Leicester outfit will very soon have a branch of its own. A marvellous scheme involving local residents, many who had never volunteered on a rail revival scheme before, has rebuilt the branch linking Swithland sidings to the edge of the Mountsorrel granite quarry,

Above: Heavy freight was a big revenue earner for the Great Central Railway right up to the last years of the London Extension, and there are many, including this author, who believe it should have been retained at least as a Freightliner route. Had it been, it would have definitely eased congestion to surviving trunk routes today. BR Standard 9F 2-10-0 No. 92067 is seen south of Rugby with a 'windcutter' rake of 16-tin mineral wagons in 1965. You can still see a 9F hauling a 'windcutter' on the Great Central Railway today.
MICHAEL MENSING

Left: The livery of the original Great Central Railway carriages as depicted on an Edwardian hand-coloured postcard of a Manchester to Marylebone express.
ROBIN JONES COLLECTION

Finally, there is another section of the London Extension that also has rails today: the privately owned Finmere station site, which is the subject of a separate chapter.

We also look at the extension to the Nottingham light rail metro system, which uses part of the GCR trackbed for modern trams to take people into the city centre once more; and the calls to revive the London Extension as a more environmentally friendly alternative to the controversial High Speed 2 route between London, Birmingham and the north.

Most importantly, however, in this second decade of the 21st century, the Great Central is on the move again.

At the time of writing, a £1 million appeal to raise funds for Network Rail to build a new bridge over the Midland Main Line at Loughborough, linking the two heritage Great Central railways, thereby creating a unique 18-mile inter-city steam highway between Nottingham and Leicester, was nearing its target. Great Central officials have called 2015 The Year of the Bridge.

Furthermore, there are also plans for a major new railway museum at Leicester North.

Drawn up in partnership with Leicester City Council and none other than the National Railway Museum at York, long considered to be the finest in the world, the £16 million structure would have classic exhibits from the National Collection preserved safely under cover indoors while steam trains draw up alongside.

Using the GCR(N)'s main line connection and the new Loughborough bridge, the future Greater Great Central will see charter trains arriving from all over Britain, maybe with the planned new museum as the destination.

The multiple benefits for the local economy would be immense.

Of course, like virtually everything else that had been achieved by the heritage sector over the past half century as outlined in this book, public support is required literally by the trainload – and that includes donations for the Bridging the Gap project, not to mention to associated infrastructure which includes replacing a missing embankment at Loughborough.

The GCR of the future is all set to become a significant international visitor destination.

Today's GCR is not quite what Edward Watkin envisaged, but there is no doubt if he is looking down on the phenomenal accomplishments of volunteers saving the last vestiges of his empire, he will rest very happy indeed.

Above: BR Britannia Pacific No. 90054 *Dornoch Firth* passes the site of Charwelton station in 1965. The rundown of the London Extension has begun: Charwelton station closed to passengers and goods on March 4, 1963, followed by the line itself on September 5, 1966.
MICHAEL MENSING

Left: BR Britannia Pacific No. 70013 *Oliver Cromwell* heads the first train of the Great Central Railway's Easter Vintage Festival past Woodthorpe en route to Leicester North on April 18, 2014.
GRAHAM NUTTALL

Author:
Robin Jones

Designer:
Leanne Lawrence

Reprographics:
Simon Duncan

Senior sub-editor:
Dan Sharp

Production manager:
Craig Lamb

Marketing manager:
Charlotte Park

Publisher:
Tim Hartley

Commercial director:
Nigel Hole

Publishing director:
Dan Savage

Published by:
Mortons Media Group Ltd,
Media Centre,
Morton Way,
Horncastle,
Lincolnshire LN9 6JR
Tel: 01507 529529

Printed by:
William Gibbons and Sons,
Wolverhampton

ISBN:
978-1-909128-42-2

MORTONS
MEDIA GROUP LTD

www.classicmagazines.co.uk

CHAPTER 1

Edward Watkin's
EMPIRE

Manchester, Sheffield & Lincolnshire Railway Class 2 (later LNER D7) 4-4-0 No. 567, one of the class which operated the company's express trains from Manchester to London King's Cross between 1887 and 1894 in pre-London Extension days, using the Great Northern Railway main line south from Retford.

The modern-day Great Central Railway (Nottingham) is the base of a project designed to replicate this particular locomotive.

An appropriate cylinder block has been found and a Great Central Railway tender, the frames of which are suitable for reuse, has been obtained from the Midland Railway-Butterley and taken to Ruddington, while original Kitson drawings for the class have been sourced from the National Railway Museum.

The original No. 567 was one of a class of 31 locomotives built between 1887-94 at the Kitson works in Leeds and Gorton works in Manchester. Popular and economical locomotives, they survived into the LNER era where they became Class D7. The last was taken out of service and scrapped in 1939.

The project, being undertaken under the banner of the 567 Group, involves building an all-new boiler rather than modifying an existing one.

The new locomotive will be based at today's Great Central at Loughborough, but will be available to visit other heritage lines.

Group chairman, Andrew Horrocks-Taylor, said: "These elegant 4-4-0s were the pride of the MS&LR and then contributed towards the nascent GCR's slogan 'rapid travel in luxury'. Indeed the GCR's legendary first chairman Sir Edward Watkin was so pleased with his Class 2, it was immortalised as the locomotive which features in the company crest.

"While we'll incorporate some minor changes, the new No. 567 will be externally indistinguishable from its predecessors." 567 GROUP

Manchester, Sheffield & Lincolnshire Railway Tricomposite coach with luggage compartment, built in 1876 and restored by owner the Vintage Carriages Trust in Great Central pre-Grouping livery. It is part of the collection at the trust's Museum of Rail Travel at Ingrow on the Keighley & Worth Valley Railway. *KWVR*

Sir Edward Watkin was certainly a man ahead of his time. He started building an Eiffel Tower in London.

He expanded the Metropolitan Railway, which today forms a large part of London Underground.

He dreamed of building a Channel Tunnel and having trains running from the industrial north of England straight through to Paris more than a century before anyone began seriously discussing HS2 and beyond.

He was also responsible for building the last great trunk railway of the steam era in Britain… the Great Central Railway.

Watkin was born in Salford, Lancashire, on September 26, 1819, the son of wealthy cotton merchant Absalom Watkin, a prominent radical figure in the Anti-Corn Law League.

Privately educated, he began work in his father's mill business and became a partner in it. In 1845, aged just 26, he founded the *Manchester Examiner*, a radical newspaper.

He lived at Rose Hill, Northenden, a suburb of Manchester, in a house bought by his father in 1832.

As a businessman during the years of

The six Manchester Sheffield & Lincolnshire Railway Pollitt Class D5 4-4-0s were based on Parker's last design as locomotive superintendent: although he left in 1893, the first D5 was not built until July 1895. No. 694 is pictured at an unspecified location. TONY HISGETT COLLECTION*

A portrait of Edward Watkin by Augustus Henry Fox.

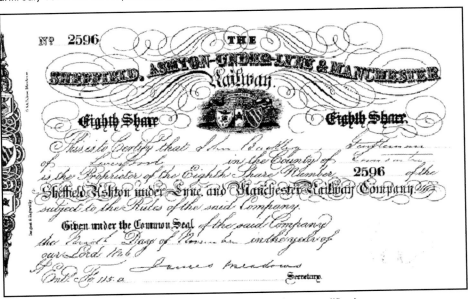

A Sheffield, Ashton-under-Lyne and Manchester Railway shares certificate.

Railway Mania, his attention, like that of many of his contemporaries, became fixed on railways, and in 1845 he became secretary of the Trent Valley Railway, the year before it was sold to the London and North Western Railway. After the sale, Watkin became assistant to Captain Mark Huish, the wily and controversial general manager of the LNWR.

Watkin toured North America and in 1852 published a book about railways in the USA and Canada.

He became secretary of the Worcester & Hereford Railway and on January 1, 1854, took over as general manager of the Manchester Sheffield & Lincolnshire Railway. He held this position to 1862, and was chairman of the company from 1864 to 1894.

In the meantime, Watkin was knighted in 1868 and made a baronet in 1880.

His involvement in railways was by no means limited to the UK. He promoted the building of

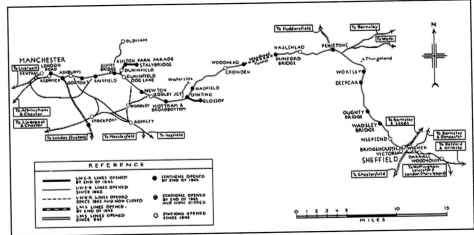

A LNER map of the original Manchester, Sheffield & Lincolnshire Railway main line over the Pennines.

The South Eastern Railway Class O 0-6-0s some of which were later rebuilt as the O1 class, were the main freight engines of the SER, and later the South Eastern and Chatham Railway for several years during the Watkin era. However, they were displaced by the more powerful C class 0-6-0s following the amalgamation of the South Eastern Railway and London, Chatham & Dover Railway in 1899. The sole preserved O1, No. 65, is seen double heading with C No. 592 on the Bluebell Railway in 1999, with a special to mark the centenary of the merger. ROBIN JONES

A caricature of Edward Watkin in an 1875 edition of *Vanity Fair*.

the Canadian Pacific Railway, helped build the main line between Athens and Piraeus and became an adviser on Britain's development of Indian railways.

In 1866 he became a director of the Great Western Railway and later took a similar position with the Great Eastern Railway. By 1881 he was a director of nine railways and trustee of a 10th. These included the Cheshire Lines, the East London, the Manchester, Sheffield & Lincolnshire, the Manchester, South Junction & Altrincham, the Metropolitan, the Oldham, Ashton & Guide Bridge, the Sheffield & Midland Joint, the South Eastern, the Wigan Junction and the New York, Lake Erie and Western railways.

However, it is the Manchester, Sheffield & Lincolnshire Railway that concerns us most here.

The MS&LR was formed in 1847 by the amalgamation of the Sheffield, Ashton-under-Lyne and Manchester Railway, which opened in 1845, with two proposed lines – the Sheffield and Lincolnshire Junction Railway and the Great Grimsby & Sheffield Junction Railway – and had its headquarters at Manchester London Road.

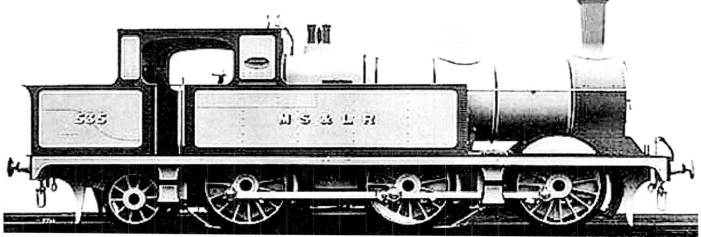

Manchester, Sheffield & Lincolnshire Railway 0-6-2T No. 535 was the first British locomotive to be fitted with a Belpaire firebox.

Laying the foundations for Marylebone station in the mid-1890s. ILLUSTRATED LONDON NEWS

In 1848, the Great Grimsby & Sheffield Junction Railway opened between Grimsby and New Holland and then extended to Market Rasen and Lincoln. The last stretch from Woodhouse Junction, near Sheffield, to Gainsborough was completed in 1849. On July 16, a special train carried the directors from Liverpool to Grimsby.

The MS&LR started digging a second bore for the Woodhead Tunnel beneath the Pennines as part of what became rapid expansion. It was completed in 1852.

The company shared Retford station with the Great Northern Railway, which granted the MS&LR running powers to London in return for access to Manchester & Liverpool. The MS&LR also had a connection with the Lancashire & Yorkshire Railway at Stalybridge, a shared station.

However, after the MS&LR appointed James Allport as manager on January 1, 1850, relations soured with the GNR. He forged a partnership with the LNWR and Midland Railway, known as the Euston Square Confederacy. The agreement gave a monopoly over the L&Y and Midland for traffic to Hull, but banned co-operation with the GNR.

Through carriages were introduced from Sheffield to London via the Midland and LNWR in 1851, and the MS&LR opened a new station at Sheffield.

Yet the MS&LR's principal source of income came from freight, mainly coal.

When Allport left to became general manager of the Midland, he was replaced by Watkin, who removed the restrictions on co-operation with the GNR, which proceeded to build on its relationship with the MS&LR and its route into Manchester.

A bitter dispute then raged with the LNWR, particularly over the use of Manchester station,

after the MS&LR cut its ties with the company. By 1858, a price war was raging for both passengers and freight, but a peace deal was eventually reached.

In 1862, the MS&LR and LNWR jointly leased the Oldham, Ashton and Guide Bridge Railway.

Meanwhile, private investors had floated the Cheshire Midland Railway and the Stockport & Woodley Junction Railway. Ignoring objections from the LNWR, the MS&LR supported the scheme and in 1860 the Stockport, Timperley & Altrincham Junction Railway was proposed.

The GNR mooted the revival of an earlier scheme for a line between Garston and Liverpool, and became a partner in the above-mentioned two, along with the West Cheshire, when they gained parliamentary approval in 1861. This group of lines became the Cheshire Lines Committee.

While Watkin was on the other side of the Atlantic involving himself with the Grand Trunk Railway of Canada, some MS&LR directors met with their Midland counterparts who wanted a way into Manchester and agreed to share their line from New Mills. This move scuppered Watkin's aims for closer ties with the LNWR and GNR that would solve the MS&LR's financial problems, and he duly resigned his post, although remained a major shareholder with a seat on the board.

However, he returned as chairman in 1864, and the following year the Midland became the company's third partner, running in 1866 from Rowsley through New Mills into Manchester London Road, a missing link which gave it a route to London.

In the Victorian era, Watkin developed into something of a latter-day Isambard Kingdom Brunel, who linked his GWR at Bristol to New York via his steamships *Great Western* and

Great Britain. Watkin, by contrast, wanted to cross the sea in the other direction, to France, not necessarily by boat, but by a tunnel beneath the English Channel. His acquisition of directorships of the locality's railways – he became chairman of the Metropolitan Railway in 1875 and South Eastern Railway in the 1880s – enabled him to manoeuvre into position to make such an attempt.

He saw opening an independent route to London was crucial for the long-term survival and development of the MS&LR. However, not only would it link the north of England to the capital, but could also become a springboard for a world-shrinking rail link direct to the Continent.

By then, he not only controlled the railways from the channel coast to the big cities of the north, but was also on the board of the Chemin de Fer du Nord, a French railway company based in Calais.

EDWARD WILLIAM WATKIN, ESQ., M.P. FOR STOCKPORT.

Edward Watkin as sketched in 1864. ILLUSTRATED LONDON NEWS

Wembley Tower, Watkin's version of the Eiffel Tower, reached only its first stage before funds ran out. AUTHOR'S COLLECTION

The Victorian Channel tunnel which stretches out from Abbots Cliff is still intact, but off limits. Had history taken a different course, and Sir Edward Watkin's grandiose scheme for an intercontinental railway been allowed to bear fruit instead of being stopped by a fearful government in 1882, trains could have been running from here to Loughborough and beyond today! LEONBPHOTOGRAPHY.CO.UK *

His ambition was to run passenger trains directly from Liverpool and Manchester to Paris via a tunnel under the English Channel, and accordingly he linked up with the Submarine Continental Railway Company.

He also decreed that the main line of his railway, including the future route to London, should be built to a wider loading gauge to accommodate continental trains.

Jumping ahead for the moment, herein lies a long-held urban myth that the route later known as the Great Central Railway was built to today's Berne loading gauge, and could therefore accommodate modern Channel Tunnel trains if it was still open. This is not the case: the Berne loading gauge was not specified until 1912, 15 years after the route opened.

In 1880-81, the South Eastern Railway began digging a pilot at Shakespeare Cliff between Folkestone and Dover, and tunnelled 6211ft using a 7ft diameter boring machine. On the other side of the channel, the French tunnels reached 5476ft from Sangatte.

The scheme set alarm bells ringing over fears of an invasion from France. The War Office Scientific Committee, Lord Wolseley and Prince George, Duke of Cambridge, opposed the tunnel for this reason, and Queen Victoria reportedly found the concept to be "objectionable". Try as he might, Watkin did not muster sufficient support to stop the project from being blocked by the Board of Trade in 1882 and cancelled in the interests of national security.

The original entrance to Watkin's tunnel remains in the chalk cliff face but is now closed off for safety reasons.

He then considered a similar tunnel beneath the Humber, and the MS&LR made trial borings at South Ferriby, matching similar work undertaken by the North Eastern Railway at North Ferriby. However, the empowerment of the Hull & Barnsley Railway made the Humber tunnel project an economic non-starter.

Watkin did not rule out the idea of channel shipping as a moneymaking venture. As South Eastern Railway chairman, he supported a scheme by the Lydd Railway Company to use the vast amount of shingle at Dungeness in Kent to build a deep water port on the cheap, creating a new holiday resort in the process.

The Lydd Railway Company's branch from Appledore to Dungeness opened to Lydd on December 7, 1881, and throughout on April 1, 1883. A second branch was opened the following year from a point just south of Lydd to New Romney. The railway's terminus was next to Dungeness lighthouse, which it served by a siding.

Promoters of the port scheme hoped that Dungeness could be served by cross-channel steamers running to the small French fishing port of Le Tréport, 114 miles from Paris. However, the scheme came to nothing.

At the same time, the Cheshire Lines Committee had been steadily expanding. In 1874, it opened Liverpool Central station, reached through a 1320-yard tunnel, and in 1877 built a temporary station at Manchester Central, approached by a 1¼-mile viaduct. A permanent station was opened in 1880, and the Midland switched its services to it, eventually building a direct line from Chinley.

As demand for coal boomed during the Victorian era, competition between railways to carry it stiffened. The MS&LR invested heavily in extra sidings, relief tracks and station improvements, but a line of its own to London still remained the ultimate goal.

Expansion of the company's network continued and in 1889 permission was granted for a line from Beighton, where the MS&LR crossed the Midland, to Annesley, north of Nottingham. For the company, this was a major turning point, for it unlocked the way for a line to London of its own.

At first, MS&LR trains via Annesley ran into the GNR's Nottingham London Road station.

In 1890, the GNR rejected Watkin's idea of a MS&LR line from Nottingham to the Metropolitan which extended to Aylesbury in 1892.

Despite struggling for money, the MS&LR submitted a Bill for this extension to London in 1891, with a new terminus at Marylebone.

The GNR, Midland and the LNWR vociferously opposed it, as did artists in St John's Wood and the cricketers of Lords. Although agreement was reached with the cricketers, with the railway building a cut-and-cover tunnel under Lords, the artists predicted it would create "a line for the conveyance not only of passengers, but of coal, manure, fish and other abominations".

Others expressed their doubts too. Both the Midland Railway and GNR believed that the cities and major towns of Britain were by then well served by one if not more railways, and why build a new trunk line replicating the services of similar routes? That view would dog the then-

Steam-hauled passenger services returned to Wembley Park, a station opened by Sir Edward Watkin, for a series of special trips on August 16, 2014, to mark the 150th anniversary of the Chesham branch. Alongside the platform stands Bill Parker's GWR 2-6-2T No. 5521, in its cut-down cab identity as L150. ROBIN JONES

Metropolitan Railway E class 0-4-4T No. 1 which dates from 1898, heads a complete rake of wooden-bodied stock, not unlike the daily mode of transport in Watkin's day, at Moorgate station on January 10, 2013, the first day of London Transport Museum's phenomenally successful public steam trips through the tube tunnels to mark the 150th anniversary of the Underground. Watkin hoped to use the Metropolitan Railway as a link in his grandiose scheme to build an intercontinental line from Liverpool to Paris via a Channel tunnel. ROBIN JONES

new railway in various shapes and forms throughout its existence.

Indeed, in 1896, the Light Railways Act had been passed, enabling basic lines like the Kent & East Sussex, Mid-Suffolk and East Kent light railways to be built, using barebones infrastructure to link rural communities not considered to be economically worthwhile by the major railway companies to the national network, and running at a maximum speed of 25mph. Made famous by Colonel Holman F Stephens who built up an empire of such lines, in many ways these 25mph operations were the ancestors of today's heritage railways.

At the same time, the first road motor vehicles were making an appearance, marking the start of an era where eventually railways would lose their monopoly of public transport.

The Bill failed at its first stage in the House of Commons, but Watkins produced support from both the Metropolitan and the South Eastern railways along with various Sheffield manufacturers. Also, the MS&LR began buying objectors' houses in London, and resubmitted the Bill, which finally gained Royal Assent in 1893.

Watkin, whose health was deteriorating retired in 1894 at the age of 74 and moved to his home in North Wales, resigning the chairmanship of his various companies.

So he was not in charge to see the opening of the MS&LR's London Extension to passengers in 1899.

By then, no longer was his former company a trans-Pennine route linking Manchester to Derbyshire, Nottingham and Grimsby. It had transformed itself into a major national transport provider,and changed its name to reflect its new position.

No longer would the provincial city of Manchester be its home – it moved its headquarters to the new showpiece terminus at Marylebone.

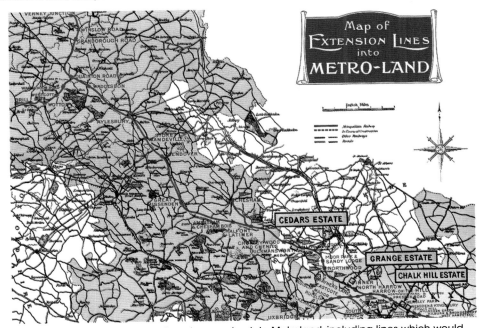

The Metropolitan Railway's westward expansion into Metroland, including lines which would link to the Manchester, Sheffield & Lincolnshire Railway's London extension.

Outside railways, Watkin was Liberal MP for Great Yarmouth (1857–1858) Stockport (1864–1868) and Hythe in Kent (1874–1895). He was High Sheriff of Cheshire in 1874.

Watkin's final project was his bid to replicate the Eiffel Tower at Wembley.

An identical-looking 1200ft tower – 111ft taller than the Paris counterpart was designed as the centrepiece of a large public amusement park intended to entice London residents on to his Metropolitan Railway.

The park opened in 1894 and Watkin built a new station – subsequently much enlarged – at Wembley Park.

The tower, dubbed Watkin's Folly, and which would have been the world's largest man-made structure, reached the first level,

154ft above the ground, by the end of 1894, but the project hit financial turbulence, and the foundations were found to be unstable.

Never officially opened to the public, nonetheless it attracted a steady stream of tourists for more than a decade, until it was demolished by dynamite in 1907.

The site became occupied by Wembley Stadium, complete with the twin towers.

Watkin's son Alfred Mellor also served as a director of the MS&LR from 1875-77 and 1899-1900, and was also MP for Grimsby.

Edward Watkin died on April 13, 1901, and is buried in St Wilfrid's churchyard in Northenden, where a memorial plaque commemorates his life. ∎

CHAPTER 2

The last trunk route of the steam age

Sir Douglas Fox, who oversaw the building of much of the southern section of the London Extension.

"If you see a bandwagon, it's too late," is a famous quote from the late financier James Goldsmith. He should know, because his business acumen made him a billionaire.

By 1893, when the Manchester, Sheffield & Lincolnshire Railway received Royal Assent for its 92¼ mile London Extension, there were already four trunk routes linking London to the Midlands and the North – the Great Northern, Midland, London & North Western and Great Western railways.

Indeed, only one town on the London Extension – Lutterworth – was not already served by railways.

By the 1890s, most of the national railway network was in place, and while the aforementioned minimalist light railways tried to mop up the remote areas left without a rail link, the general way forward was then by and large to improve the existing railways in terms of speed, comfort and capacity rather than build more and double up on routes.

The MSLR wanted a slice of London action, but that was all it would ever get – a slice. Its 92 mile extension from Annesley to Marylebone was very much late in the day as far as the national rail network was

concerned. As such, despite its many advantages, it was destined to lag behind the existing trunk routes, which had established their own regular patronage, at least in passenger terms. And this single inherent major flaw was ultimately to prove the downfall of the route.

In spite of the voicing of such criticisms and objections, the MSLR pressed ahead.

The first sod of the London Extension was cut on November 13, 1894, by MSLR chairman the Earl of Wharncliffe at Alpha Road, London, near to Lord's Cricket Ground, officials of which had earlier tried to hit the MSLR's plans for six.

When we look back to the building of the first great inter-city and trunk lines such as the Liverpool & Manchester, Brunel's Great Western and the London & Birmingham railways, we see those wonderful sketches of armies of navvies hewing great cuttings out of the ground with nothing more than advanced than picks and shovels.

By the time of the London Extension, technology had moved on: the navvies were still very much there, but their efforts were aided by earth-moving machinery such as mechanical excavators.

A suburban shuttle heads out of Marylebone, as depicted in an Edwardian hand-coloured postcard. The Manchester, Sheffield & Lincolnshire/Great Central livery evolved under the reigns of its locomotive superintendents. Sacre used Brunswick green livery with reddish-brown frames during his tenure from 1859-86. Small panels were lined with black and a white edge, while cab sides, tank sides, and tenders were edged with a wide black band and vermilion edge. Extra white lines were used on express passenger locomotives. Parker simplified this scheme and removed much of the lining. Boiler bands were black, which was also used for panel edging. During the early 1890s, the green was lightened from Brunswick green to chrome green, with frames and valances painted brown.
ROBIN JONES COLLECTION

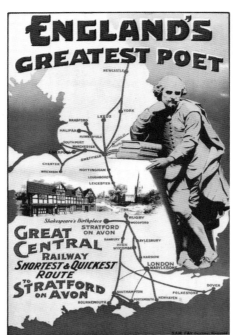

Contractors' railway lines run alongside the stupendous 21 arch Brackley viaduct as it takes shape in the summer of 1895. By this time, the availability of steam-driven earth-moving equipment made the building of such trunk routes far easier than in the embryonic days of the railway network, when navvies had only picks and shovels to carry out their tasks.

Belgrave & Birstall station north of Leicester was typical of the island platform design of station on the London Extension. It is a rare example of a station that was demolished rather than restored in preservation.
BEN BROOKSBANK*

BUILDING THE LONDON EXTENSION

Designed for high-speed running throughout, the London Extension ran from Annesley, north of Nottingham, to Quainton Road in Buckinghamshire. From there, the route followed the Metropolitan Railway's Buckinghamshire extension as far as Harrow-on-the-Hill. From a point near Finchley Road, a new line ran into the terminus at Marylebone.

The northernmost section of the London Extension, from Annesley to Rugby, was supervised by Sir Edward Parry. The southern and Metropolitan sections were overseen by brothers Sir Douglas Fox and Francis Fox of the firm Sir Charles Fox and Sons.

Sir Douglas was also involved with the construction of the Snowdon Mountain Railway and worked on several of London's early tube lines including the Great Northern and City, and the Hampstead lines. Francis Fox was a consultant for the Simplon Tunnel and in 1878 constructed the replacement train shed at Bristol Temple Meads station. Both worked on the building of the Liverpool Overhead Railway, which opened in 1893.

Unlike many of the earlier trunk route and main lines, the London Extension crossed rolling agricultural land for most of its length. However, it involved several major engineering works, not least of all in crossing the densely populated parts of Nottingham and Leicester.

In Nottingham, streets of slum houses were demolished to make way for the line, and there as well as in Leicester, the GCR built new housing estates to replace them. A major new city centre station, Nottingham Victoria, was also built.

Boring tunnels through the sandstone on which much of Nottingham is built presented problems, and buildings above had to be shored up while work was in progress.

In Leicester, the line was taken through the city on a lengthy brick viaduct and a series of bridges. At Leicester Central, a Roman mosaic pavement was discovered, and a large hall was built beneath the station so it could be preserved in situ.

At Rugby, a viaduct took the London Extension over the LNWR's West Coast Main Line. Eight miles to the south, the Northamptonshire hills were penetrated by the 2997 yard Catesby Tunnel.

More viaducts were built at Swithland Reservoir, Brackley, where a stupendous 21 arch structure soared above the field, Braunston,

Staverton and Catesby, along with many miles of substantial cuttings and embankments.

Building the London Extension cost £11.5 million, nearly double the original estimate, and almost bankrupted the GCR.

However, it had the advantage of being built to very high standards, with a ruling gradient of 1-in-176, curves with a minimum radius of a mile through the rural areas and only one level crossing between Sheffield and Marylebone – all of which made the route perfect for fast running and competing with the older rivals whose routes were slightly shorter.

Again, it was hoped that if a Channel tunnel were given the green light, the London Extension could steal a march on other companies' routes as it was built to a wider loading gauge to accept continental trains in that event. Indeed, the standardised design of stations, nearly all being built to an 'island' design with one platform between the two tracks instead of the conventional two at each side, would allow the tracks to be moved further out if Watkin's dream was ever realised and continental trains were to run over the route. Stations would therefore not have to be rebuilt or redesigned in that event, or if extra tracks were needed at a later date.

MARYLEBONE STATION

It was originally planned that Marylebone should have eight platforms, but the building costs were far higher than was anticipated, and in view of the colossal overspend on the London Extension, only four were built, three within the train shed and one, platform four, west of the train shed. Indeed, economy was the only order of the day when it came to building the station.

Indeed, the GCR had become so short of money by that stage that the only way it could obtain locomotives and rolling stock for the London Extension was to establish a separate trust company and buy them on hire purchase.

Marylebone was the last of the major London termini to be opened. As such, the company was always going to have difficulty competing against the longer-established stations, even though its express trains were often more luxurious, boasting state-of-the-art coaches with electric lighting, and restaurant and buffet cars on most services..

The station was designed by Henry William Braddock, a civil engineer employed by the railway. Its design follows the neo-baroque Renaissance revival style, employing warm brick and cream coloured stone, and harmonising with surrounding buildings with Dutch gables.

Again, because of the huge expense of the London Extension, the adjoining Great Central Hotel was built by a different company, but was tastefully linked to the booking office by an attractive coach gate.

Despite the economy measures, when building a new London terminus, it was impossible to escape the expenditure, as happened in Nottingham and Leicester, of having to build replacement homes for those demolished to make way for the railway. Remember that when Paddington station was built by the GWR half a century before, it lay in green fields. Marylebone in the 1880s was a different matter entirely. A total of 507 homes occupied by 3073 people had to come down, and were replaced by the six five-storey blocks known as Wharncliffe Gardens after the railway's chairman.

Much of the land was bought in readiness for the time when extra platforms were needed. That day never came.

The neo-baroque frontage of Marylebone station today. ROBIN JONES

Above: The lettering on the original gates at the entrance to Marylebone. ROBIN JONES
Left: A late Victorian sketch of the Marylebone booking hall.
Right: The Great Central Railway Hotel at Marylebone. ROBIN JONES

The station was officially opened on March 9, 1899. Three special trains ferried in northern guests from Manchester, Sheffield and Nottingham, with 734 people enjoying a six course lunch in a marquee.

The head of the Board of Trade, Charles Thomson Ritchie, 1st Baron Ritchie of Dundee and a future home secretary, opened the station and the London Extension. In his speech, addressing the issue of whether London needed another railway connection to the North, he said that all of the existing lines suffered from,

"enormous congestion." The upper storey of Marylebone station was occupied by offices, a boardroom and a committee room, allowing the GCR headquarters to be moved from Manchester London Road to Marylebone in the middle of 1905.

Marylebone acquired a second railway line in 1907, when the Bakerloo line was extended from Baker Street.

The new Marylebone underground station took the name Great Central until 1917, when it was changed to Marylebone.

Horse-drawn cabs line up alongside Great Central trains to ferry passengers from inside Marylebone station to the heart of the capital. ROBIN JONES COLLECTION

The Marylebone trainshed today is a terminus for Chiltern Railways services from Birmingham, but its platforms are never as packed as those at King's Cross, Paddington or Euston. ROBIN JONES

Manning Wardle 0-6-0ST No. 1212 of 1891 *Sir Berkeley* was supplied new to contractors Logan & Hemingway and used on the construction of the Beighton-Chesterfield section of the Manchester, Sheffield & Lincolnshire Railway. A popular performer in preservation, it is pictured at Barrow Hill in April 2012. HUGH LLEWELLYN*

THE LONDON EXTENSION OPENS

The London Extension was opened for coal traffic on July 25, 1898, and for passengers on March 15 the following year. That day, the first GCR passenger express left Marylebone.

The contrast with the opening of early trunk routes could not have been more dramatic. When George Stephenson's Liverpool & Manchester Railway opened in 1830, it seemed as if most of the populations of both cities turned out. However, on that historic first train out of Marylebone, at 5.15am, only four passengers were aboard.

The next train, the 9.15am, attracted 14 passengers, and the one afterwards, at 1.15pm, 34 turned up. The 5.15pm evening dining car express had only 15 first-class passengers who booked reserved seats.

The Railway Magazine reported at the time that these numbers were "regarded as eminently satisfactory". However, the passenger take-up was at best slow, a factor that would forever dog the London Extension.

The goods yard at Marylebone was not opened until April 11, 1889, because of the huge amount of work needed to erect a gargantuan warehouse to serve it.

The GCR was still very much a Sheffield-oriented company, and kept many of its traditions intact even when it ran into the capital. Services to London were referred to as Down trains, the opposite of standard practice on every other main line to the capital.

MAP OF GREAT CENTRAL MAIN LINE

The route of the great Central Railway from Manchester to Marylebone.

MANCHESTER
Sheffield
Annesley
East Leake
Aylestone
Rugby
Woodford
Brackley
Grendon Underwood
LONDON MARYLEBONE

FORWARD

The Great Central Railway's western main terminus, Manchester Central station was designed by Sir John Fowler and built by engineers Richard Johnson, Andrew Johnston and Charles Sacre between 1875-80 by the Cheshire Lines Committee. The station's roof is a single span wrought-iron truss 550ft long with a span of 210ft and standing 90ft high above the tracks. Officially opened on July 1, 1880, in 1963 it was awarded Grade II* listed building status for its special architectural or historic interest. ROBIN JONES COLLECTION

MANCHESTER SHEFFIELD AND LINCOLNSHIRE RAILWAY
TRESPASSERS ON THIS PROPERTY WILL BE PROSECUTED

Great Central Railway general manager Sam Fay.

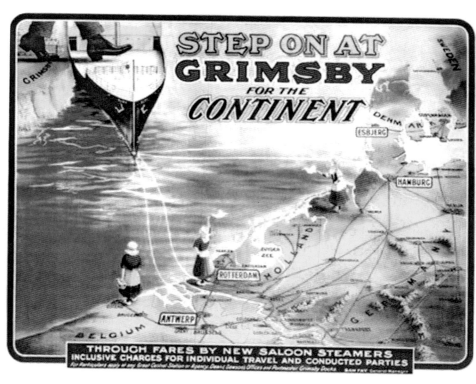

A SECOND GCR ROUTE INTO LONDON

The GCR also ended up with a second route into the capital, offering somewhat of a parallel alternative route to a southern portion of the London Extension.

In 1898, when relationships between the GCR and the Metropolitan Railway were becoming increasingly fraught, particularly with regard to the imminent sharing of tracks at the southern end of the London Extension, the former looked at an alternative line into the capital, bypassing the tracks it planned to share from Quainton Road southwards. The GCR wanted to make sure that the Met could not exercise a stranglehold over its London Extension services.

The GCR found a willing partner in the Great Western Railway, and set out to build a new joint line from north of Quainton Road to Northolt Junction, which lay on the new GCR line to Neasden Junction and had been authorised by the Great Central Act of August 12, 1898.

On August 1, 1899, the Great Western and Great Central Railway Companies Act authorised the Great Western & Great Central Joint Railway, which was also known as the Alternative Route.

The joint line saw major upgrading of the GWR route between High Wycombe and Princes Risborough in order to handle the extra traffic from the GCR. A junction was created on the London Extension at Greatmoor to the east of Grendon Underwood and a link to Princes Risborough, joining the GWR at Ashendon Junction, was constructed.

At the southern end of the joint railway, another new line was built from High Wycombe via Beaconsfield, Gerrards Cross, Denham and Ruislip to Northolt Junction. There it divided: the northern path was the GCR's link to Neasden, and southern path ran on to the GWR main line via Greenford.

Opened in 1906, the joint line provided a second option for GCR inter-city expresses. However, by that time, the GCR had long since patched up its differences with the Metropolitan Railway, and furthermore, the new pair of the latter's double tracks, which had been laid from Neasden to the approach to Marylebone, had been ceded in 1903 to the GCR when the route was quadrupled: thereafter, the GCR was no longer at the mercy of the Met.

SIR SAM FAY

Soon after Marylebone opened, Lord Wharncliffe resigned through illness and died a few days later. He was replaced by director Alexander Henderson, who had done much to facilitate the completion of the London Extension by raising funds for the purchase of locomotives.

In 1900, William Pollitt was superseded as general manager by Sir Sam Fay, a career railwayman who joined the London & South Western Railway as a clerk in 1872, and in 1892 had been placed in charge of the ailing Midland & South Western Junction Railway.

Headhunted by the GCR, Fay began his tenure by extending through passenger services between Newcastle and Bournemouth, supplemented by express excursions between Nottingham, Leicester and Bournemouth using the Woodford Halse to Banbury branch.

He also reintroduced services between Sheffield and Leeds via the Swinton & Knottingley Joint Railway, as well as through services from Marylebone to Stratford-upon-Avon.

Under his wing, journey times for expresses between Marylebone and Sheffield were cut to three hours, a reduction of eight minutes at an average speed of 54.9 mph.

He established a publicity department, the first of its kind in the modern railway world, in 1902, and introduced the first weekly zone season tickets in Manchester in 1904.

Also in 1904, the GCR bought travel agents Dean & Dawson and the Cleethorpes Promenade Pier Company and acquired the Wrexham, Mold & Connah's Quay, the Buckley and the North

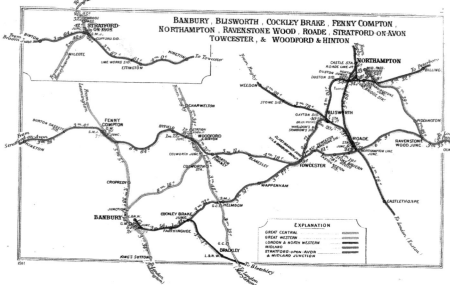

A Railway Clearing House map showing Woodford Halse at the heart of a network of lines linking to the London Extension, including the Great Central's Banbury branch.

The Manchester, Sheffield & Lincolnshire Railway, which included the Grimsby Docks Company, built up a substantial shipping fleet including North Sea and Humber ferries. The Great Central continued the flow of investment in new ships for all services. Pictured is the company's *SS Bury*. At the start of the First World War, the Germans seized three GCR ships in the Hamburg area, and several others were requisitioned by the UK government. Four were lost during the conflict. ROBIN JONES COLLECTION

Wales & Liverpool railways. Fay's appointment brought about a rapid thaw in the icy relations with the Metropolitan Railway, leading to the lease of the Canfield Place to Harrow line by the GCR and, the Uxbridge branch apart, the switching of all Met lines beyond Harrow to a new Metropolitan and Great Central committee.

The GCR continued to expand. In 1907, it added the Lancashire, Derbyshire & East Coast Railway to its growing portfolio, and a new coal traffic concentration yard situated at Wath began operations.

Under Fay, several joint lines were created in and around South Yorkshire – the GC Hull & Barnsley & Midland, the GC and Midland, the Gowdall & Braithwell and also the South Yorkshire Joint.

Between 1910-14, the expansion of the GCR empire peaked, the jewel in the crown being the opening of Immingham Docks, as outlined in Chapter 4. The last big extensions included the Doncaster avoiding line and the opening of the separate Mansfield railway.

In 1913, Fay became a part-owner of the struggling Freshwater, Yarmouth & Newport Railway. Two years earlier, Fay had been invited by Secretary of State for War Richard Haldane to join the Ports and Transit Executive Committee, which comprised the managers of six principal railway companies to examine the problem of feeding London in the event of enemy action on the south coast.

When war broke out, Fay and eight other managers of leading railways became part of the Railway Executive Committee chaired by the LSWR's Herbert Walker, as the Government took control of the nation's railway network for the first time.

The GCR played a significant role during the war, with up to nine special coal trains for Navy purposes run on a single day from South Wales to Immingham.

At the beginning of 1917, Fay took over the post of Director of Movements at the War Office, yet he refused to wear a military uniform or to shave off his beard, even though the post carried

the rank of general. In March 1918, he succeeded Sir Guy Granet, the Midland Railway's general manager, as Director-General of Movements and Railways, with a seat on the Army Council. During this absence from the Great Central, Fay's assistant, E A Clear, took charge of the day-to-day running of the system. Fay went back to the GCR in May 1919.

THE GROUPING

The Government relinquished control of the railways in 1919, but there were calls for the system to be permanently nationalised, for reasons of greater efficiency through pooling resources and eliminating duplicate routes, making the most of benefits realised from the wartime years of central control. However, a

halfway house compromise was reached with the Railways Act 1921 enacted by the government of David Lloyd George, whereby the 120 railway companies were 'Grouped' into just four, the Great Western, the Southern, the London Midland & Scottish and the London & North Eastern railways.

The GCR became part of the latter from January 1, 1923, and its directors held their final meeting on December 15, 1922, during which a decision was taken to award Fay a pension of £3000 a year.

After regaining control in 1919, the GCR had steadily restored its services. By the middle of 1921, all of the through services had been restored and the longest of all, the Aberdeen to Penzance train, was introduced.

A Great Central Railway first class kitchen car for use on the expresses over the London Extension. ROBIN JONES COLLECTION

THE TWO BRANCHES

The London Extension had just two passenger-carrying branches. At Woodford Halse, where the GCR created an important railway centre, there was a connection with the East & West Junction Railway, which was later incorporated into the Stratford-upon-Avon & Midland Junction Railway.

The connection at Woodford Halse North Curve Junction allowed the GCR to serve the town of Shakespeare's birthplace, boasting that it could get there faster than its rivals.

To the south lay Culworth Junction, from where the GCR built an 8¾ mile branch running south-west to Banbury's GWR station, originally named Banbury Bridge Street. It allowed many important cross-country workings to take place.

The Aberdeen to Penzance Express used the Woodford Halse to Banbury branch of the GCR through Banbury, as did the 'Ports to Ports Express', between Newcastle-upon-Tyne and Middlesbrough, and Cardiff and Newport as well as sleeper services between the North East and Bournemouth, Southampton and Swindon.

Indeed, this GCR branch made Banbury as important as London termini in its day, boosting

the town and its cattle market. Woodford Halse station was a variation on the standard island platform design typical of the London Extension, being reached from a roadway (Station Road) that passed beneath the line.

Serving what was, in effect, a four-way junction, it was provided with a more extensive range of platform buildings and facilities beneath a longer awning.

A separate platform was provided on the west side for Stratford-upon-Avon & Midland Junction trains, a timber structure later replaced by a concrete slab version.

To the north of the station, a major locomotive depot housing up to 30 locomotives with space to double that number, also wagon and sheet repair shops, plus extensive marshalling yards, were located.

Much of the depot was built on top of a 35 acre embankment formed mainly from spoil that had been taken from Catesby Tunnel a few miles to the north.

Roads containing 136 terraced dwellings to house the railway workers were built on the east side of the embankment, together with a street of shops, a cinema and railway workers'

social club. Woodford Halse, which had previously been a small rural village, became the GCR's 'mini Crewe', with a population of around 2000.

Woodford Halse became famous for its intense freight workings, handling fish from Grimsby and Immingham and steel from the cutlery-making capital of Sheffield, which was the hub of the GCR system.

While the London Extension crossed several railways, it did not have physical connections with most of them.

A JUNCTION AT LOUGHBOROUGH?

Few people today are aware that Loughborough Central very nearly became a junction station in its own right, serving a short branch planned by GCR to link it to the booming 19th century industrial centre of Shepshed five miles away.

In 1883, the 10 mile Charnwood Forest Railway from Ibstock to Loughborough via Shepshed opened. Linked to the LNWR at Ibstock, it formed an extension to the Ashby & Nuneaton Joint Railway, part of which is preserved today as the Battlefield Line.

The Loughborough terminus lay in Derby Road, and gave the town its only Station Street, despite it eventually having two far more important stations.

The Charnwood line ran up huge losses, compounded by financial irregularities and fraud among its officials. The LMS withdrew the loss-making passenger services in 1931. Freight continued until October 31, 1955, when services between the Charnwood Granite Company's siding in Shepshed and Derby Road were withdrawn.

The Derby Road station has long since been demolished, but the brick-built goods shed survives, and the nearby Station Hotel became a pub.

Despite the loss-making Charnwood line, the MSLR planned to build a branch from the London Extension to Shepshed, and parliamentary powers were obtained for a new line, the Loughborough & Shepshed Railway.

It was planned to leave the Charnwood railway near Shepshed and climb to Loughborough at a higher level with a station near Derby Road, but high enough to allow it to bridge the adjacent main road.

From there, it would have crossed the Midland Railway by a bridge before joining the GCR to the north of Loughborough Central.

However, after the London Extension opened, the Shepshed branch scheme went on to the back burner and the statutory powers were allowed to lapse. The plans were revived briefly in 1905, with the main line connection this time south of Loughborough Central, but again nothing came of it.

After the completion of the London Extension, the GCR did build a two mile freight-only branch from the main line between Nottingham and Leicester, along with a set of sidings, to serve the limestone (plaster) works of the Gotham Company's works (later British Gypsum) in the small settlement of Gotham itself. The branch closed in May 1969.

Above: Pre-paid newspaper parcel stamp from the Great Central Railway.

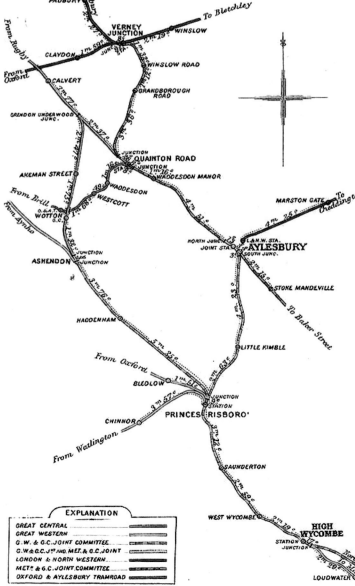

Right: Railway Clearing House map showing the complexity of lines where the Great Western & Great Central Joint Railway diverged from the London Extension at Grendon Underwood Junction.

The early years of the Great Central Railway and the London Extension saw emphasis placed on long-distance trains. This postcard view shows Class 11B 4-4-0 No. 1022 heading an express from Manchester near Harrow, the coaching stock having been designed by Parker for the London Extension. In 1896, the directors had agreed on a coach livery of grey upper panels and dark brown lower panels, replacing it in 1902 with cream upper panels. Varnished teak was reintroduced in 1908. ROBIN JONES COLLECTION

TRAFFIC LEVELS

The London Extension's main competitor was the Midland Railway, which had served the route between London, the East Midlands and Sheffield since the 1860s.

Passenger traffic was slow to establish itself on the London Extension, and enticing customers away from the existing trunk routes into the capital was more difficult than the GCR had anticipated.

It did appeal, however, to high-end business customers, through the company's promotion of its services as 'Rapid Travel in Luxury'.

However, passenger loadings on the London Extension were rarely described as heavy. One exception was special event days at Wembley Stadium, which had opened in 1923 on the site of Watkin's Tower, when extra trains were laid on to cope with demand.

Indeed, Marylebone became renowned for its quietness when compared with the other great London termini. Most of the revenue came from freight, not passenger workings, of which there were only 14 arrivals each day in 1903, in an age when railways were still far and above the premier form of transport.

Coal was the staple income for the GCR, which built up trade from carrying ironstone, steel, gypsum and limestone, as well as newspapers, mail and parcels. Extensive sets of sidings were provided at each station, with holding sidings at various points where the main line was met by a private railway, such as the Mountsorrel quarry branch north of Rothley.

The locomotive sheds that provided the motive power for the freight workings were Annesley, Woodford Halse, Banbury, Leicester and York.

The GCR did steal a march on its rivals during the First World War, when it by and large maintained the prewar timetable and did not axe its restaurant cars, or slow the crack expresses too often. Indeed, GCR passenger traffic peaked at 34 million in 1918.

During the conflict, the hotel at Marylebone became a convalescent home.

Those who used the luxury coaches praised them as equal to anything that Pullman cars could offer.

The most famous named train on the GCR was 'The Master Cutler'. It had its origins in the early years of the GCR when a special train from Marylebone to Sheffield was nicknamed the 'Sheffield Special'. It would have run to Leeds Central but for an injunction sought by competitors.

In the early years of the London Extension, emphasis was placed on developing long-distance traffic rather than local services. The busiest section for local traffic eventually became Nottingham to Leicester, with 12 trains a day. Local services were principally Nottingham to Leicester, Nottingham to Rugby, Nottingham to Woodford Halse, Leicester to Brackley and Woodford Halse, and between Leicester, Nottingham and Sheffield.

These local trains were hauled by anything from tank engines to retired express passenger types. At one stage, three Brush steam railcars were briefly introduced on services between Leicester, Rugby and Loughborough.

One of the busiest depots was Neasden, which supplied locomotives for the heavy London suburban traffic and routes as far north as Woodford Halse, with subsheds at Marylebone and Aylesbury. Neasden provided locomotives for use on the Wembley specials, and a loop line was built around the newly-constructed stadium to facilitate the extra movements required.

The big advantage of the London Extension was the ability of trains to cover long distances without being interrupted. This aspect led to the use of the route for the abovementioned cross-country services as well as the development of long heavy coal trains, later known as 'windcutters' which comprised huge rakes of 16 ton mineral wagons. ∎

An Edwardian postcard view of the front of Nottingham Victoria, the new station built by the Great Central Railway for its London Extension. ROBIN JONES COLLECTION

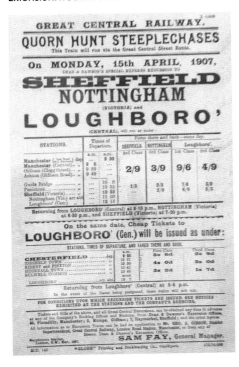

CHAPTER 3

Robinson's locomotive fleet

A hand-coloured postcard view of GCR 8B 4-4-2 No. 363 heading an express train.

Facing a potential rise in passenger traffic, the Great Central Railway placed an order for two pairs of different locomotives – one pair being the Class 8C 4-6-0, the other this Atlantic type.

The two locomotive types borrowed heavily from Robinson's Class 8 and shared as many common components as possible to allow easy conversion of the 8Bs to the 4-6-0 configuration.

However, due to a much smaller than anticipated traffic increase, no further Class 8Cs were built, and instead 25 more Class 8Bs were ordered and built between 1904-6. They had larger fireboxes as there was no longer a need to convert the locomotives to a 4-6-0.

The last class member was withdrawn in 1950. ROBIN JONES COLLECTION

Robinson Class 11B 4-4-0 No. 107 emerged from Vulcan Foundry as works No. 1920 in April 1904.

The 11B was Robinson's second design since assuming the mantle of GCR locomotive engineer. It was his first express engine design and 40 were built between October 1901 and June 1904.

The order for the first 30 was placed with Sharp Stewart and the last 10 with Vulcan. No 107 was the fourth of the Vulcan engines and was supplied at a cost of £3050.

Robinson's first design for the company was the 9J 0-6-0 goods engine which became known as the 'Pom-Poms' due to

their fierce staccato exhaust which was said to resemble the pom-pom naval gun fitted to Royal Navy ships. When the 11Bs came out, they were soon known as the 'bogie Pom-Poms'.

Their main duties were taking over the expresses on the London Extension from the Pollitt 4-4-0s which had worked the line since its opening in 1899.

This photograph was taken at Neasden in 1913. At the Grouping, No. 107 was located at Retford shed but by the dawn of BR, it was to be found at Trafford Park. It was withdrawn as LNER No. 2329 in February 1949.

JOHN CRAWLEY COLLECTION

In 1902, John George Robinson was appointed as chief mechanical engineer of the Great Central Railway, and launched an era of classic designs which both ran alongside and then superseded the best of the Manchester, Sheffield & Lincolnshire types.

Under Robinson, the Great Central rapidly became famous for 4-4-2s and 4-6-0s, the latter also being used for fast freight traffic. His remit was clear: to produce faster express passenger locomotives for the main line to London, while designing a range of engines for heavy freight work as the company expanded across the northern industrial belt.

Robinson was born in Bristol on July 30, 1856, and was educated at Chester Grammar School. In 1872, he started work as an apprentice engineer at the Great Western Railway's Swindon Works under Joseph Armstrong and William Dean.

In 1878 he became assistant to his father Matthew Robinson, the GWR's divisional locomotive, carriage, and wagon superintendent at Bristol. Matthew had worked for the Newcastle & Carlisle Railway and knew the early steam locomotive pioneers the Hackworths.

A major step up the ladder came in 1884 when he joined the Waterford & Limerick Railway as its locomotive, carriage and wagon assistant superintendent. He was promoted to superintendent the following year.

He joined the GCR in 1900, firstly as locomotive and marine superintendent at Gorton Works, before adding the carriage and wagon

Class 9N (LNER A5) 4-6-2T No. 165 emerged from Gorton Works in March 1911. It was withdrawn by British Railways in August 1959 from 40E Colwick shed, the year before the last of the class, Robinson's last passenger tank design, came out of traffic.

Designed to haul suburban services out of Marylebone, the GCR built three batches between 1911-17. A fourth batch was ordered by the GCR, but was built after Grouping in 1923. The LNER ordered a fifth from Hawthorn, Leslie & Company for use in the North Eastern area. A total of 44 were built.

The A5s were among the first GCR locomotives to have superheaters. The first locomotives had Schmidt types, but Robinson applied changes as he evolved his own superheater design.

Robinson's Superheater expanded the superheater elements into the smoke header, and had a combined blower and circulating valve to protect the elements from the firebox gases when the regulator was closed. From 1948, Thompson L1s replaced the A5s on Marylebone services. The surplus A5s were moved to Lincolnshire.
ROBIN JONES COLLECTION

Harry Pollitt became locomotive superintendent of the Manchester, Sheffield & Lincolnshire Railway in 1893, just before the company built its London Extension and changed its name to the Great Central Railway.

For the extension, he built several 4-4-0s and his last design, the six Class 13 (LNER X4) 4-2-2 singles. This class survived into LNER ownership, and was the final single driver express locomotive of any pre-Grouping company to operate scheduled services in Britain.

On the extension, they were replaced by Robinson D9s in 1903, and moved to Cheshire where they successfully worked express trains. All six survived into LNER ownership, only to be withdrawn between 1923-7. The four superheated boilers were kept as stationary boilers.

Pollitt resigned in 1900, and married an Australian lady at Marylebone church.

His father, Sir William Pollitt was the general manager of the MS&LR/GCR from 1886 until 1903.
ROBIN JONES COLLECTION

Sacre Class 12AT 2-4-0T No. 450 was built by the Manchester, Sheffield & Lincolnshire Railway at Gorton in March 1881, and is seen at Neasden shed on July 1, 1922.

The class had double frames and raised running plates to give clearance to the outside cranks, the Sacre cab with its oval side windows and, in this picture, a Robinson chimney which replaced the stovepipe type fitted by Parker, which in turn had replaced Sacre's original design.

Eight of these engines were built between December 1880 and April 1881. Only two, Nos. 450B and 449B, became LNER property at the Grouping.

In November 1912, No. 450 was placed on the duplicate list and given the letter 'B' after its number. In April 1914 it was fitted with the apparatus for working motor trains - pulleys, rods and whistle mounted on the cab roof - at which time it became Class 12AM.

It was through push-pull duties on various branch lines that its survival was ensured until withdrawn in January 1925 as LNER Class E8 still carrying its GCR number 450B despite having been allocated LNER No. 6455.
JOHN CRAWLEY COLLECTION

department to his remit two years later and being promoted to the top job.

Robinson's first passenger locomotive design for the GCR was Class 11B (LNER D9) 4-4-0. Forty were built between 1901 and 1904, the last being withdrawn by British Railways in 1950.

He followed this in 1913 with the larger Class 11E (LNER D10) Director 4-4-0s for express trains from Marylebone to Sheffield Victoria and Manchester London Road. Ten were built, followed by 11 Class 11F (D11) Improved Directors during 1920-1924.

Possibly best known of all, if only for the sole British-based survivor's exploits on the modern-day GCR, is his 8K (O4) heavy freight 2-8-0.

It was introduced in 1911 and many were built especially for the Railway Operating Division of the Royal Engineers in 1917 and saw wartime service overseas.

It was outstandingly successful – and has been hailed as the locomotive that won the First World War.

Its boiler proportions were held to be excellent while its somewhat minimalist design, lacking in sophistication, meant that poor maintenance was all but unheard of.

The last O4 was withdrawn by British Railways in 1966.

Further designs included the six-coupled express engine *Sir Sam Fay*, the express 4-6-0

Robinson Class 1 4-6-0 No. 424 was built at Gorton in December 1912. In June 1913 it was named *City of Lincoln*. The first engine on the class was named after the company's general manager Sir Sam Fay. To locomen the class members were known as the 'Sir Sams'. Six of this class were built, but despite their massive and very handsome appearance they did not live up to expectations; first allocated to Manchester-Marylebone expresses, they were soon relegated to secondary passenger duties. They were fitted with the largest diameter cylinders (21½in) to be used in the UK. The boiler, firebox, valves, and inadequate driving axleboxes all played their part in their poor performance.

They were fitted with 4000 gallon tenders with a coal capacity of six tons. No. 424 is pictured in May 1914 on a servicing road off of the turntable at Manchester Central. It was withdrawn as LNER No. 5424 in November 1945.
JOHN CRAWLEY COLLECTION

Class 8A No. 1177, built at Gorton in July 1910, was an example of Robinson's first eight-coupled design and was intended for working heavy coal trains over the Pennines.

Of massive appearance, they soon acquired the nickname of 'Tinies'.

The first of them appeared in November 1902 and the last in February 1911. During this time 89 engines were built, the first three by Neilson, 51 by Kitson and the remaining 35 at the GCR's Gorton Works.

After grouping a number of engines were transferred over to the Great Northern section of the LNER and were well received by the men. There they were designated Class Q4.

This class were the only eight-coupled engines to work regularly over the Midland & Great Northern Joint Railway.

This photograph of No. 1177 was taken at Annesley shed on July 21, 1923. The locomotive was withdrawn as LNER No. 3241 in April 1950.
JOHN CRAWLEY COLLECTION

Robinson Class 11E 4-4-0 No. 437 *Charles Stuart Wortley* was built at Gorton in November 1913 and allocated to Neasden shed, where it was employed on the London-Manchester express, displacing the 'Sir Sams' (Sir Sam Fay class) which had proved disappointing.

The 11Es were successful engines and ranked as one of Robinson's best designs. They were fitted with 4000 gallon tenders with a coal capacity of six tons.

They were known as Directors as each was named after a company directors. Wortley was elected to the board in 1897 and served throughout the existence of the company up to December 31, 1922. Ten in all were built, all between August and December 1913.

During 1920, No. 437 was renamed *Prince George* in honour of King George V and Queen Mary's fourth son (Prince George, Duke of Kent, who died in 1942). On February 27, 1927, it collided with a Lancashire & Yorkshire 2-4-2 double ender tank engine at Penistone. The damage was such that No. 437 had to be rebuilt incorporating new frames. Pictured at Neasden on June 6, 1922, it was withdrawn as British Railways No. 62658 in August 1955. JOHN CRAWLEY COLLECTION

Robinson Class 9Q 4-6-0 No. 36 was built by the Vulcan Foundry, works No. 3418, in September 1921. These four-cylinder engines were a mixed traffic version of Robinson's 9P (Lord Faringdon class) having 5ft 8in driving wheels in place of the 6ft 9in of the 9P.

Many derogatory remarks have been made about this class which was Robinson's last 4-6-0 design. While they were used on fast goods and excursion traffic tasks which they performed very successfully, the main reason for complaint was their voracious appetite for coal which resulted in them being given the nickname of black pigs.

Altogether, 28 engines of this class were built during 1921-22 with a further 10 outshopped after the Grouping under the auspices of the LNER. Would this have happened if they had really been all that bad?

No. 36 is pictured on June 6, 1922. It was withdrawn as LNER No. 1363 in June 1948.
JOHN CRAWLEY COLLECTION

goods engine *Glenalmond*, and the six-coupled large tank engine with Robinson superheater.

The four-cylinder express passenger engine *Lord Faringdon* was another noteworthy superheated locomotive.

His special 0-8-4T shunting locomotives were built for pushing loaded trains over the humps at the shunting and marshalling yards at Wath, near Doncaster. They were one of the first British locomotives to be provided with three high-pressure cylinders.

His superheater design earned him a diploma at the Latin-British Exhibition of 1912, and he also designed a successful lubricator for locomotive and marine engine use.

Robinson laid out the company's new carriage and wagon works at Dukinfield, and was responsible for enlarging and modernising the locomotive works at Gorton.

It has been said that his best locomotives

were produced by 1914. Critics have said that while Robinson's 8Ks and Atlantics, which had the same boiler, were good machines, and the Directors were also successful, the 4-6-0s were left wanting, largely because of poor air access to their grates.

Robinson was awarded a CBE in 1920 for his work as a member of the Railway War Manufacturers' Sub-Committee.

He was also a member of the Institution of Civil Engineers and the Institution of Mechanical Engineers.

At the Grouping of 1923, Robinson was offered the job of chief mechanical engineer of the new London & North Eastern Railway, but declined in favour of the younger Nigel Gresley, his counterpart at the Great Northern Railway.

As of December 31, 1921, the company's locomotive fleet comprised 909 tender engines and 452 tank engines. ∎

Robinson also introduced the first 2-6-4Ts to Britain, in the form of his Class 1B (LNER L1/L3), of which 20 were built between 1914-17.

While several railways introduced large tank engines to haul heavy goods and mineral trains, they tended to lack sufficient braking power and fuel capacity.

Based on the M1 0-6-4T, they were fitted with boilers similar to those on the Director 4-4-0s. This necessitated the fitting of a leading pony truck. Inside cylinders and piston valves were fitted. Not one of Robinson's most attractive designs, they were quickly nicknamed 'Crabs'.

Designed to haul coal traffic from pits in Nottinghamshire and Derbyshire to Immingham Docks, their braking deficiencies soon became noticed.

They were accordingly relocated to lighter duties very quickly, such as short colliery trips, pick-up goods and even some passenger services.

The last was withdrawn by British Railways in 1955.

No. 272 is pictured newly outshopped at Gorton Works.

ROBIN JONES COLLECTION

Robinson 9P 4-6-0 No. 1165 *Valour*, one of only six engines of this class, was built at Gorton in July 1920 and is pictured at Leicester coal stage on June 9, 1923, still in GCR livery.

As built they were fitted with four cylinders, the inside ones driving on the leading axle, those on the outside on the centre axle.

Stephenson link motion was employed driving all four cylinders from the same set of motion via rocking levers. They were provided with 4000 gallon tenders with a coal capacity of six tons.

The name *Valour* remembered GC staff who died for their country between 1914-18.

One of its nameplates is now in the National Railway Museum at York.

Normally the engine works plates were carried beneath the nameplates on the sides of the splashers, but on this engine, the sole example, they were fixed to the cylinder covers. Every November 11 up to the outbreak of war in 1939, *Valour* would work the 8.20am from Manchester London Road station to Sheffield conveying a party of railway employees to a memorial service. It was withdrawn from traffic as LNER No. 1496 in December 1947.

JOHN CRAWLEY COLLECTION

Sacre Class 6B 4-4-0 No. 442 was built at Gorton in October 1878. Built with double frames, the class were graceful looking engines with their running plates curved upwards to miss the outside cranks and their distinctive cabs with oval side windows. A total of 27 engines were built, the first in May 1877 and the last in July 1880.

No. 442 was provided with a tender carrying 1800 gallons of water and 2¾ tons of coal. It was not only the first of its class to be fitted with the automatic vacuum brake but also the last of its class to be taken out of service.

In September 1914 it was given the suffix B, becoming No. 442B, as its number was required for fitting to a new Class 1A engine built in September that year. In January 1922 it was given a general repair at Gorton and sent to Annesley shed for working DIDO trains. Annesley shed employed more than 500 staff and was located out in the wilds. Virtually no housing was available, the nearest villages being Hucknall and Bulwell, both some miles off. This meant that the company had to provide a service to enable them to get to work.

This it did, running many trains every day of the year, day in, day out – hence DIDO. The company used the oldest engines and coaches for this service and at the time that No. 442B was so employed, six-wheeled coaches were the order of the day.

Previous to its general repair in 1922 it had been shedded at Leicester and although transferred to Annesley for the DIDO service, this photograph shows it again at Leicester on June 9, 1923. Its long life was no doubt due to it working the DIDO service which was an easy job, not accumulating a high mileage. It was withdrawn as LNER No. 6464 in March 1930.

JOHN CRAWLEY COLLECTION

CHAPTER 4

Immingham Dock
and the GCR's electric tramway

Gateshead tramcar No. 10, pictured at Beamish museum, was once Grimsby & Immingham No. 26. ROBIN JONES

Immingham Dock in North East Lincolnshire is now Britain's busiest bulk cargo port by tonnage. It handles up to 55 million tons a year, including nearly 20 million tons of oil and 10 million tons of coal.

With river and in-dock deep-water facilities and easy access to the major trade routes, Immingham Dock is less than 24 hours from a European market of 170 million people. An extensive range of freight services serves northern Europe, Scandinavia, and the Baltic.

It therefore remains one of the Great Central Railway's biggest success stories.

Coal was the reason for its existence. The Manchester, Sheffield & Lincolnshire Railway's premier east coast port was Grimsby, but it had to be shared with the booming North Sea fishing fleet, and so expansion for trade was limited.

The development of the South Yorkshire coalfield in late Victorian and Edwardian times led to a demand for bigger and better export facilities. The North Eastern and Hull & Barnsley railways were able to ship coal through the rapidly expanding port of Hull.

The MSLR had looked at building a new deepwater port at Killingholme west of Grimsby in 1874, but failed to take the idea any further. A site next to Grimsby docks was

Former Gateshead & District Tramway cars at Immingham Dock in 1958. BEN BROOKSBANK*

considered and rejected in 1900, because it would have needed constant dredging of the approach channel.

In 1903, the GCR chose Immingham, two miles to the east of Killingholme, and a year later obtained parliamentary powers to build the dock, which lay at the point where the Humber deepwater channel came close to the shore and would not need more than basic dredging.

The docks was designed by Sir John Wolfe Barry & Partners and built by contractors Price, Wills & Reeve of Edinburgh, and equipped by Rowlandson & Ball.

The first sod was cut on July 12, 1906, an event witnessed by 682 special guests who arrived in four trains from Marylebone, Manchester, Sheffield and Cleethorpes.

The docks took six years to build, with

The entrance to Immingham Dock with the dock offices right, as pictured on a Great Central postcard. ROBIN JONES COLLECTION

An original Great Central Railway postcard view of the then-new Immingham Dock and one of its locomotives hauling coal wagons. ROBIN JONES COLLECTION

3½ million cubic yards of earth excavated.

The completed project had 170 miles of sidings capable of holding 11,600 wagons and was able to export 56,000 tons of coal each day. Needless to say, it had impeccable GCR rail connections.

Immingham Dock was opened by George V and Queen Mary on July 22, 1912, after they arrived on a Humber ferry, which had steamed through the entrance lock. GCR general manager Sam Fay was unexpectedly knighted on the steps of the dock's general offices during the ceremony for the achievement.

Around the dock today, there are still reminders of its proud GCR past, such as Robinson Road and Henderson quay.

THE GRIMSBY & IMMINGHAM ELECTRIC RAILWAY

The massive new docks, which had been built in the middle of flat marshes and pasture land by the Humber, needed a workforce, and one had to be shipped in on a daily basis from Grimsby.

A Light Railway Order for a link between the dock estate and Grimsby was obtained. Rather than build a traditional steam branch line, the fact that shift workers would be using it round the clock required a cheap and effective means of running regular services day and night. By now, electric trams had proved their worth in London and elsewhere, and cheap electricity could be supplied from the Immingham power plant.

The tramway was, however, very different from those which sprang up in Britain's cities at the time, and indeed was the country's sole example of a US-style 'inter urban' electric line.

The tram replaced a Great Central steam railcar service that ran on the parallel Grimsby District Light Railway originally laid by the dock contractor. The tramway was inspected on November 22, 1911, and initially opened for traffic on May 15, 1912, to Immingham Town. The final section to Immingham Dock's eastern jetty opened on November 17, 1913.

The Immingham Dock-Town line was a double track set on its own reserved way but becoming a street tramway once reaching Immingham. Trams reversed towards Grimsby and the line and, once on their reserved way, maintained a south-eastward course across the

marshes on a near straight five-mile stretch to Pyewipe depot.

From the depot, the line veered to the right to become a street tramway, using Gilbey Road and finally Corporation Road. A waiting room and parcels office were built next to Corporation Bridge as the Grimsby terminus.

In addition to the 7¾ mile main line, the system also included a short Immingham branch to serve the new GCR locomotive depot and a station was opened in Queens Road near the footpath linking the line to the depot.

The railway used four types of single-deck bogie tram. Firstly, there were 12 54ft-long trams designed by the GCR and constructed by Dick Kerr of Preston. They were the longest non-articulated trams Britain.

Four short trams, bought for operations in Grimsby's streets, were scrapped in the early 1930s.

Three trams were bought from Newcastle Corporation in 1948 but were scrapped in 1957.

A total of 18 trams dating from the 1920s

were bought from Gateshead and District Tramways in 1951. These were painted in British Railways electric locomotive green.

The tramway closed on July 1, 1961, despite carrying 950,000 passengers a year, with services replaced by buses. By then, trams were out of fashion, with most city networks having closed. British Railways was seeking to eradicate 'one-offs' in its portfolio wherever possible.

Four Grimsby & Immingham tramcars have survived into preservation. The most unusual is a four-wheel trailer tower wagon, which has been preserved at the Crich Tramway Village.

One of the original GCR cars, No. 14, has been preserved as a part of the National Collection, and is also based at Crich. In July 2012, it revisited Grimsby for the docks' centenary.

Two of the ex-Gateshead cars survive. One of them is preserved at Crich as Grimsby & Immingham No. 5, and another, Grimsby and Immingham No. 26, is preserved at Beamish museum and operates as Gateshead No. 10. ■

Original GCR tramcar No. 14 (right) with Gateshead No. 5, at Crich on May 2011.
PAUL JARMAN

CHAPTER 5

The Grouping, British Railways, Beeching and beyond

The raw power of a BR standard 9F 2-10-0 hauling a rake of 'windcutter' mineral wagons: No. 92031 passes Charwelton in 1963. This magnificent class is represented on today's Great Central Railway. MICHAEL MENSING

So much about the original Great Central was excellent, especially its fast and efficient service to London, boosted by a slick publicity department, but despite constant improvements in its fortunes, it never scaled the heights of its northern rivals.

As a constituent of the LNER, the Grouping brought an increase in freight traffic from the south Midlands and south-west England. However, the LNER was dominated by Great Northern thinking, and the King's Cross to Newcastle and Edinburgh East Coast Main Line was therefore considered its primary north-to-south route.

The First World War and the hostile European political climate in its aftermath finally and firmly quashed any lingering hopes of the GCR main line being linked to a steam-era Channel tunnel. An attempt to rekindle the scheme had been blocked in the 1920s.

Fast and convenient it might be, but the GCR main line was always considered by the LNER as a secondary route.

That did not mean it was relegated to backwater status. On the contrary, by the end of the Thirties – considered by many to be the last great decade of the UK steam age, with long-distance passenger trains to the fore – there were six expresses a day from Marylebone to Sheffield, calling at Leicester and Nottingham, and going forward to Manchester.

A London to Sheffield timing of three hours and six minutes in 1939 placed it on a level pegging with the rival LMS service on the Midland route out of St Pancras.

Yet again, it was only special events in the capital, such as those held at Wembley Stadium that saw the route realise the levels of patronage that GCR shareholders had originally hoped for. The British Empire Exhibition in

1924/25, for instance, had trains running non-stop every 10 minutes.

During the Second World War, a flying bomb hit Marylebone signalbox, killing two men, and the goods warehouse was destroyed in a Luftwaffe raid in April 1941. The station was closed for seven weeks after a bomb penetrated one of the tunnels.

NATIONALISATION

Britain's railways were again placed under state control during the Second World War, and this time calls for the arrangement to become permanent were heeded. Indeed, years of wartime neglect and under investment left the nation's railways in a parlous state, and Nationalisation was seen not only as the best but the only way out.

After January 1, 1948, the Great Central lines became part of the Eastern Region of British Railways. It thrived in the early years of

Pictured in LNER livery, Robinson Class 8B 4-4-2 No. 261 was built by Beyer-Peacock as works No. 4601 in July 1904 at a cost of £3750. As saturated steam engines, their performance was considerably enhanced by superheating, which started with No. 361 in March 1912 (No. 261 was dealt with in September 1920) and continued until January 1936 when No. 1004 (6004 by then) was the last engine to be so fitted. The class proved to be one of the major workhorses of the GCR and were thought highly of by the men who nicknamed them 'Jersey Lillies' after Lillie Langtry, the actress and mistress of Edward VII. GCR general manager Sam Fay was very keen on promoting excursion traffic, and with a view to attracting publicity, he arranged for a return tour from Manchester to Plymouth via Woodford, Banbury, Didcot, Bristol and Exeter, a distance of 373 miles, using only one engine and crew. No. 261 was chosen for this working, which took place over the weekend of October 28, 1904. It all went as planned with No. 261 behaving impeccably. Its standard 4000 gallon tender managed to accommodate an extra ton of coal over its usual capacity of six tons. This photograph – taken at its home shed of Leicester on June 9, 1923 – shows the loco still carrying its GCR numberplate on the cabside and lettered LNER. No. 261 was not to receive its new number until February 1925 when, like all GCR engines, it had a '5' added to the front of its number, becoming LNER No. 5261. It was withdrawn as LNER No. 2906 in November 1941. JOHN CRAWLEY COLLECTION

LMS Jubilee 4-6-0 No. 45638 Zanzibar heads the 8.38am express from Marylebone at Nottingham Victoria in 1962, with a LNER L1 2-6-4T waiting on the middle line. BEN BROOKSBANK*

Heading a Down Manchester express, Gresley A3 Pacific No. 60063 Isinglass awaits departure from Marylebone's Platform 4 in 1956. BEN BROOKSBANK*

Nationalisation, until freight traffic, which was its life blood, began to decline, and competition from cheaper and more versatile road haulage began to have a serious effect on its business.

Services to High Wycombe and Princes Risborough were concentrated at Marylebone rather than Paddington, giving a boost to the London Extension.

In the winter timetable of 1947, the LNER had introduced the famous-named train 'The Master Cutler' over the GCR main from Sheffield Victoria to Marylebone, calling at Nottingham Victoria and Leicester Central. It was continued by the Eastern region.

The train, which included a restaurant car and was usually hauled by an LNER A3 Pacific, initially left Sheffield at 7.40am, the return journey departing Marylebone at 6.15pm.

In 1958, the GCR main line was designated as a duplicate of the Midland Main Line.

Accordingly, it was reallocated to the London Midland Region, and herein lay the roots of its demise as a trunk route to the capital.

In railways, old company loyalties and enmities died hard.

The GCR, both before and after the Grouping, had been a fierce competitor of the Midland Railway and its successor, the LMS. Now Midland men at last had their rival in their hands; it was clear who the winner would be. GCR traffic was switched to the preferred Midland route, with passenger services being run down, and also in 1958, the name 'The Master Cutler' was switched to a new all-Pullman service from Sheffield Victoria to King's Cross using the East Coast Main Line. It called only at Retford in both directions, and was diesel hauled.

In 1960, the through expresses from Marylebone to Sheffield and Manchester were withdrawn, replaced by a lacklustre semi-fast service linking Nottingham and London.

Among the services discontinued that year was 'The South Yorkshireman,' a nine-coach service started by British Railways in May 1948. Including a restaurant car, and also often hauled by an A3, it left Bradford Exchange daily at 10am, taking five-and-a-half hours to reach Marylebone. It returned from London at 4.50pm, and called at Huddersfield, Sheffield, and Leicester, and also at Halifax, Brighouse, Penistone, Nottingham, Rugby and Aylesbury for several years.

Marylebone station found itself on an international stage in 1964, at the height of Beatlemania. In April that year, the 'Fab Four' were seen dashing onto a train at the terminus pursued by an army of screaming fans, in scenes for their first movie, A Hard Day's Night. Other railway scenes were filmed on the Minehead branch, now the West Somerset Railway.

Banbury station was a meeting place of two cultures – GWR and LNER – where cross-country trains from the GCR main line arrived via the branch from Woodford Halse en route to the south and west. A father and his two children admire V2 2-6-2 No. 60893 as it stands alongside GWR 4-6-0 No. 6390 *Aldersley Hall*, on September 22, 1960. Sadly, the V2 would be scrapped just over two years later. MICHAEL MENSING

THE BEECHING AXE

Britain's railway network reached its maximum extent after the First World War, extending to 23,440 miles. However, by then, motor transport had become established, with cars, buses and lorries increasingly nibbling away at the railways' monopoly.

In the aftermath of the First World War, vast amounts of military vehicles were sold off as army surplus, allowing servicemen returning from the Western Front to set up their own haulage businesses in competition with the railways.

Swathes of branch lines and light railways that had been set up under the 1896 Act either lost their passenger services or closed completely in the late Twenties and Thirties, when it may be said that the shrinkage of the network began. Around 1300 miles of passenger lines closed between 1923 and 1939.

War-weary Britain was not ready to follow countries like the US and modernise its railway system, and so rather than opt for all-out dieselisation and electrification, the new British Railways stood by the tried and tested formula and continued to build steam locomotives.

A total of 999 British Railways Standard locos were built in the 1950s.

However, closures began again after the dust from the conflict settled. The first official withdrawal of passenger services by the new British Railways were those from Woodford & Hinton station, on the London Extension to Byfield, on the Stratford & Midland Junction Railway, on May 31, 1948. Woodford & Hinton station was renamed Woodford Halse on November 1 that year.

In 1949, the British Transport Commission's branch lines committee was

formed with the aim of closing the least-used branch lines. Lopping off loss-making services was naturally seen as a means of keeping the country's railway in profit, which they were until the mid-Fifties.

Ownership of motor vehicles grew at an annual rate of 10% between 1948 and 1964. In the Fifties, rail traffic remained steady, but the national network saw labour costs rising faster than income, and rail fares and freight charges frozen by the Government as an anti-inflation measure.

The British Railways Modernisation Plan of 1955 called for the eradication of steam and its replacement by diesel and electric traction. It led to a rush by manufacturers to build an assortment of diesel types, some of which were so unsatisfactory that they did not even survive in service until the end of steam in 1968, others disappearing shortly afterwards.

LMS 'Black Five' 44894 carries a wreath as it heads past the site of the closed Culworth station on the last day of services over the London Extension – September 5, 1966. MICHAEL MENSING

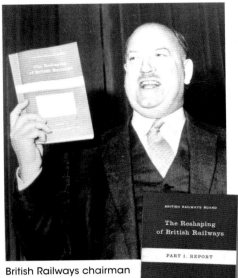

British Railways chairman Dr Richard Beeching holds up a copy of his infamous report on February 27, 1963.

Among the potential replacements for steam which were trialled over the UK network was GT3, English Electric's experimental gas turbine-mechanical 4-6-0. It appeared in early 1961, looking far more like a steam engine than a diesel, and was based to an extent on a Class 5 steam design. The culmination of 15 years design work, it impressed in trials on the Great Central main line and over Shap on the West Coast Main Line, but was high on fuel consumption, and its reversing mechanism was inadequate. It is seen passing Ashby Magna between Rugby and Leicester at 4.11pm on September 21, 1961, on its down test run. Sadly, this distinctive locomotive was not saved for posterity and was scrapped in early 1966. MICHAEL MENSING

In 1955, following the re-election of Anthony Eden's Conservative Government, the Associated Society of Locomotive Engineers and Firemen (ASLEF) called a strike over a pay increase, which amounted to the price of a packet of cigarettes a week.

It lasted from May 20-June 14 and brought British industry to a standstill. During the dispute, the millions of people who travelled by train were forced to make other arrangements, and many of them found that the alternative transport was better…and never returned to the railway. UK government transport policy

then switched from rail to roads.

By the end of the decade, British Railways was seriously in the red, and drastic measures were needed.

A total of 3318 miles of railway were closed between 1948 and 1962. The 1959 closure of the entire Midland & Great Northern Joint Railway route, linking the East Midlands with Norfolk, sent shock waves through the system. Eradicating poorly patronised branch lines was by then accepted practice, but to lose an entire system…

While there were specific events and

LONDON
(Marylebone)
AND
SOUTH YORKSHIRE

WEEKDAYS
June 5th to September 23rd inclusive

THE MASTER CUTLER

		a.m.				p.m.
Sheffield (Victoria)	-	dep. 7 40	London (Marylebone)	-	dep.	6 15
Nottingham (Victoria)	-	,, 8 43	Rugby (Central)	-	arr.	8 6
Leicester (Central)	-	,, 9 A 18	Leicester (Central)	-	,,	8 31
Rugby (Central)	-	,, 9 A 46	Nottingham (Victoria)	-	,,	9 4
London (Marylebone)	-	arr. 11 A 25	Sheffield (Victoria)	-	,,	10 11

A—On Saturdays July 1st to August 26th inclusive departs Leicester 9.22, Rugby 9.52 and arrives Marylebone 11.35 a.m.

THE SOUTH YORKSHIREMAN

		a.m.				p.m.
Bradford (Exchange)	-	dep. 10 0	London (Marylebone)	-	dep.	4 50
Huddersfield	-	,, 10 35	Aylesbury	-	,,	5 49
Sheffield (Victoria)	-	,, 11 27	Leicester (Central)	-	arr.	7 0
		p.m.				
Nottingham (Victoria)	-	,, 12 30	Nottingham (Victoria)	-	,,	7 33
Loughborough (Central)	-	,, 12 52	Sheffield (Victoria)	-	,,	8 35
Leicester (Central)	-	,, 1 11	Penistone	-	,,	9 3
Rugby (Central)	-	,, 1 39	Huddersfield	-	,,	9 33
Aylesbury	-	arr. 2 s 30	Bradford (Exchange)	-	,,	10 14
London (Marylebone)	-	,, 3 29				

S—Saturdays only

Seats can be reserved in advance at a fee of 1⁄ per seat from Bradford (Exchange), Huddersfield and Sheffield (Victoria) to London FROM Marylebone seats can be reserved at any London terminal station

RESTAURANT CAR EXPRESSES

Gresley A3 Pacific No. 60059 *Tracery* heads 'The South Yorkshireman' two miles north of Lutterworth in 1956. MICHAEL MENSING

The Locomotive Club of Great Britain's circuitous 'Thames, Avon and Severn Rail Tour' of October 12, 1963 from Waterloo to Paddington via the West Midland ran over the GCR Banbury branch to Woodford Halse, before taking the Stratford-upon-Avon & Midland Junction line. Heading it over this section were LSWR T9 'Greyhound' 4-4-0 No. 120, which by then had been preserved as part of the National Collection and repainted in the pre-Grouping company's livery, and Southern Railway Maunsell U 2-6-0 No. 31790, which was withdrawn two years later and did not survive. MICHAEL MENSING

decisions which undoubtedly hastened the demise of much of the UK network, rail closures were at the time becoming increasingly commonplace throughout the western world, as railway revenue was lost to the more versatile road transport alternatives.

Transport Minister Ernest Marples had business interests in roadbuilding companies and contracts, and was therefore accused of being biased about railways. British Railways began to fight back, and in 1961 appointed 43-year-old high-flying ICI executive Dr Richard Beeching as its chairman, with a remit to stem the company's soaring and unacceptable losses.

Beeching did not invent rail closures: during his first two years in the job, he merely rubber-stamped such recommendations from divisional managers. Many such

recommendations included the closing of intermediate stations on main lines to eliminate stops and speed up services: Belgrave & Birstall, Rothley and Quorn & Woodhouse, for instance, were closed in 1963. The Chesterfield loop closed on March 4 that year, and long-distance freight services were withdrawn from the GCR main line shortly afterwards.

Beeching did not set out to destroy railways: indeed, many historians now affirm that he saved an ailing system by judicious pruning under the narrow remit he was given by Marples.

His approach was to start with a blank sheet of paper, see what the railways could do better than road transport, allow them to do it, and vice versa.

On March 27, 1963, he delivered the biggest shock to the system with his 148-page report, The

Reshaping of British Railways – immediately dubbed the "Beeching Axe". The report called for the closure of 5000 out of a total of 18,000 route miles, 30% of the network, along with 2363 stations, 55% of the total.

While in opposition, Harold Wilson's Labour party made much of the Beeching closures, promising everyone, especially the unions, that it would sack him and reverse them if it was elected.

After the Conservative Government lost the General Election of 1964, Marples was replaced as Transport Minister by Labour's Tom Fraser, and soon afterwards Barbara Castle.

Labour did not sack Beeching as promised. Over the next six years, the Wilson Government not only implemented his recommendations, but closed more routes beyond those in his report.

LMS Royal Scot 4-60 No. 46125 *3rd Carabinier* passes Grendon Underwood Junction in 1964. MICHAEL MENSING

LMS 'Black Five' 4-6-0 No. 45215 at Amersham with a Marylebone to Woodford Halse stopping train in 1959. BEN BROOKSBANK*

Beeching is popularly blamed for rail closures, yet he did not have the power to axe any of them. The final decision rested with the transport minister, who, in some cases, exercised their power to overrule the recommendations.

One major plank of his philosophy was the change of emphasis to an inter-city network, which involved the closure of main lines that 'doubled up', as with the 1959 closure of the Midland & Great Northern Joint Railway system.

The biggest single Beeching closure was that of the London Extension, again seen as duplicating the Midland Main Line.

During the 1950s, passenger uptake on the GCR, which ran through large tracts of countryside, was lost to road transport, while the Midland route served significant urban areas.

It had been hoped that the route could be improved for parcels and goods traffic, but Beeching decided that the Great Central traffic could easily be served by other lines linking London to the north.

His closure recommendation was followed by widespread debate, especially as in February 1964, Britain signed an agreement with France for the building of the Channel Tunnel.

A letter from Denis Anthony Brian Butler, the 9th Earl of Lanesborough, published in the Daily Telegraph on September 28, 1965, read: "…surely the prize for idiotic policy must go to the destruction of the until recently most profitable railway per ton of freight and per passenger carried in the whole British Railways system, as shown by their own operating statistics.

"These figures were presented to monthly management meetings until the 1950s, when they were suppressed as 'unnecessary', but one suspects really 'inconvenient' for those proposing Beeching-type policies of unnecessarily severe contraction of services…

"This railway is, of course, the Great Central, forming a direct continental loading-gauge route from Sheffield and the north to the Thames Valley and London for Dover and France".

INSIDE THE 'KREMLIN'

Ironically, many of the Beeching closures and the reshaping of the network were implemented from within a classic London Extension landmark – the Great Central Hotel at Marylebone.

During the Second World War, the hotel at 222 Marylebone Road again became a convalescent home, before being turned in to a military office building. Much of its original opulence was boarded or painted over.

In 1946, it was sold off for use as railway offices, and two years later became the headquarters of the British Transport commission, followed by the British Railways Board.

Staff variously nicknamed it the 'Kremlin', '222' and 'The Bunker'. Visitors described it as a grim place to visit, with endless corridors of anonymous doors.

Planned by Watkin, as part of a larger Great Central, maybe as a stopover on an international route to France, it was now being used to eradicate that company's route to London.

Home to British Rail's central planning unit, the offices included a map room.

Dieselisation was not enough to save the London Extension. In 1965, Class 37 D6742 passes Woodford Hale, beneath the bridge carrying the Stratford-upon-Avon & Midland Junction line over the GCR main line. MICHAEL MENSING

The entrance to Marylebone station in the 1960s, with the British Rail headquarters building to the left. JOHN EDSER

Woodford Halse station in 1966, the year of its closure. GEOFFREY SKELSEY*

The centrepiece was an enormous map of the British Isles with the whole of the railway system marked on it. Proposed closures were marked by one colour of pin which was changed to red after the axe fell.

In 1986, the building was bought by a Japanese company and reopened as a hotel seven years later.

In 1995, it was bought by the Lancaster Landmark Hotel Company Limited, and renamed The Landmark London. It now has a five-star rating and 300 rooms and suites.

THE AXE FALLS

The sections of the GCR main line between Rugby and Aylesbury and between Nottingham and Sheffield were closed during September 3-4, 1966. Annesley motive power depot closed on January 3 that year, and Nottingham Victoria closed on September 5.

The track was lifted between Rugby and Calvert, the line from there south to Aylesbury being retained for occasional goods use. The southern section of the London Extension between Aylesbury Marylebone, which still carried considerable commuter traffic, was retained.

The closures left only the section between Rugby and Nottingham over which diesel multiple units operated a skeleton shuttle service.

Nottingham Victoria station was closed in 1967, British Rail selling the lucrative city

centre site for shopping redevelopment. A supermarket now stands on the site: all that remains of the original station is the landmark clock tower.

As a temporary measure, trains from Rugby over the remnant of the GCR route terminated instead at Arkwright Street station, a suburban stop south of Nottingham Victoria. That was ironic, because Arkwright station had been one of the stations that had been closed in 1963.

One platform was reopened to serve the six daily trains that remained.

The last train departed from Arkwright Street on Saturday, May 3, 1969. The station and viaducts carrying the railway were demolished in the mid-Seventies, and the site is now occupied by a housing development.

The line north of Nottingham remained in use until May 1968 to serve the collieries at Annesley and Newstead, but was lifted in October and November 1969.

The northern section of the GCR main line between Sheffield Victoria and Woodhouse also remained open because it also formed part of the Sheffield to Lincoln route.

Marylebone's coal depot closed in 1967 and the 28-acre goods yard was sold to the Greater London Council for housing development.

Sheffield Victoria station closed on January 5, 1970 with the closure of the Woodhead route to passengers, and trains from Lincoln were diverted into Sheffield Midland.

Above: Anti-closure slogans chalked up on an unknown Great Central line station. COLOUR-RAIL.COM

Right: The end of the Great Central: The last train departs from Arkwright Street station on May 3, 1969. DAVID HILLAS/CREATIVE COMMONS

Rugby Central in 1968, less than a year before closure. A Nottingham-bound DMU waits at the platform. DAVID HILLAS*

Left: The last train to call at Rugby Central on May 3, 1969: The station was similar in design to Loughborough Central, which survives as the headquarters of today's Great Central Railway. DAVID HILLAS*

MORE CLOSURE THREATS

In the summer of 1983, Sir Peter Parker, then chairman of British Rail, commissioned a study into a proposal to turn much of the Marylebone to Aylesbury line into a high-speed busway.

A park-and-ride station would be built near the M25 at Denham, and Marylebone would be turned into a bus station. The route was considered eminently suitable for exclusive use by buses and coaches because it had been built to a wider loading gauge.

Before he left office, Parker recommended that the findings of the study should be implemented. Meanwhile, London Midland Region managers proposed handing over the Amersham to Aylesbury route to London Underground for fourth-rail pick-up, before abandoning the lines from Marylebone to Northolt Junction and Harrow-on-the-Hill.

Aylesbury was to remain open, but all services would run into Paddington via Princes Risborough. Marylebone Station was due to close on May 12, 1986, and closure notices were duly posted there in 1984.

A legal challenge by local councils over the way in which the plans had been handled by the London Regional Passenger Committee ended up in the High Court – which upheld the committee's controversial decision not to allow British Rail to be cross-examined at a hearing over the costs of operating the threatened routes.

However, in 1986, the committee was advised by British Rail that it had made a U-turn over closing Marylebone, because of the surge in numbers of commuters at Paddington, and Baker Street had left no spare capacity. The closure threat was formally lifted on April 30 that year.

That marked the start of an £85million modernisation project for the route, which became a flagship project of Network SouthEast, with new trains and signalling and upgraded track. The ageing Class 115 DMUs were replaced by Class 165 Turbo trains, and a major modernisation programme was implemented at stations.

Following Privatisation in the 1990s, Chiltern Railways took over the route, and in 2006 two new platforms were built at Marylebone on the site of the old daytime carriage sidings.

The new platforms and partial resignalling of the station throat now make it possible to run 20 trains every hour in and out of the station.

North of Aylesbury the track remains in place, but at the time of writing, is only used regularly by waste freight trains to the landfill site at Calvert, where a junction with the Oxford to Milton Keynes and Bedford 'Varsity Line' route (which originally ran to Cambridge) remains in use.

On December 14, 2008, Chiltern Railways services were extended two miles north from Aylesbury to a new station – Aylesbury Vale Parkway – at the point where the line crosses the A41 near Berryfields Farm.

As part of the East West Rail Link plan to restore the Varsity Line, services will be extended from Aylesbury Vale Parkway via Calvert and Bletchley to Milton Keynes Central.

The Department for Transport endorsed the scheme in November 2011, with opening planned for 2019, and Chiltern providing the trains.

Once completed, passengers between Aylesbury and the Midlands or the north will no longer need to travel via London.

Further expansion plans to reconnect Aylesbury to an M6/M1 parkway station near Rugby have also been mooted by Chiltern. If that happened, it would comprise the biggest reopening of a section of the London Extension since it closed. Watkin's dreams may never have died, but are merely slumbering.

Rugby Borough Council bought the whole of the GCR trackbed through the town in 1970, and it is now a nature walk called the Great Central Way. The goods yard was used as a timber yard until the mid-1990s when houses were built on it.

The name 'The Master Cutler' survives in use. After the post-1968 Sheffield to St Pancras train lost the name, it was revived by InterCity in May 1987 for a daily service operated by InterCity 125 High Speed Trains.

When Midland Mainline took over from InterCity after Privatisation, it ran 'The Master Cutler' from Leeds to St Pancras via Doncaster and Sheffield, using a Pullman InterCity 125 set until December 14, 2008. After that, the service reverted to its post-1968 historic route, run from Sheffield to St Pancras via Chesterfield, Derby and Leicester, using a seven-car train. ∎

Right: Manchester Central station had a second lease of life between 1960-66 when it became the terminus for the Midland Pullman, the legendary streamlined blue six-coach DMU, from St Pancras. However, after the Midland Main Line between Buxton and Matlock closed in 1968, the station handled only local services to Chester and Liverpool. It closed to passengers on May 5, 1969, when the remaining services were switched to Manchester Oxford Road and Manchester Piccadilly. The grandiose Cheshire Lines Committee trainshed then fell into dereliction and was used as a car park. It was bought by Greater Manchester Council, and in 1982 was converted into the Greater Manchester Exhibition and Conference Centre (or G-Mex), which opened in 1986, and was subsequently renamed Manchester Central in honour of its railway history. The opening in 1992 of the Metrolink light rail saw trains return, in the form of modern trams. Services from south Manchester cross the railway viaduct and stop at Deansgate to Castlefield Metrolink station, running down a ramp parallel to Lower Mosley Street and alongside the south-eastern side of the former train shed, before reaching street level where they operate as trams and head towards St Peter's Square. ROBIN JONES

Seventy years after the date on the portal shows when it was built, tracks were being lifted at Catesby Tunnel. In the autumn of 2014, it was revealed that the tunnel had been acquired by a group called Aero Research Partners, which wants to convert it into an aerodynamic- performance testing facility for new Formula One cars, which would be driven through it at high speed. MICHAEL MENSING

The remains of Rugby Central today. ROBIN JONES

A new station on the London Extension! Aylesbury Vale Parkway opened to passengers on December 14, 2008. MOTACILLA*

Chiltern Railways Class 165 Turbo train No. 165035 stands at Amersham on September 8, 2013. ROBIN JONES

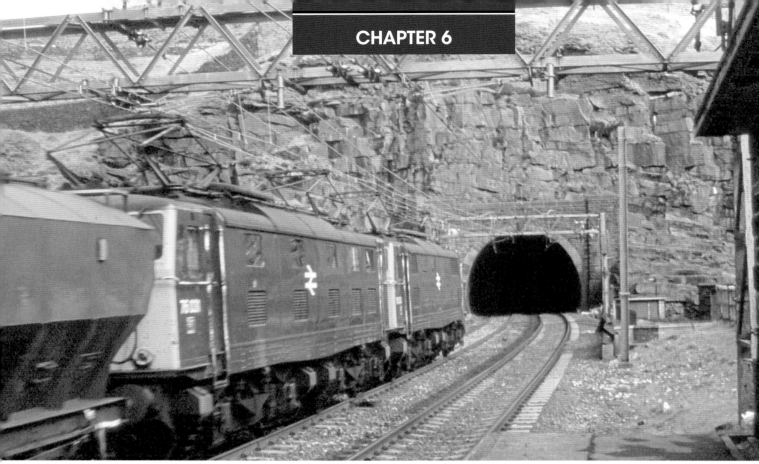

Class 76 locomotives No. 76033 and 76031 at Woodhead Tunnel on March 24, 1981. KEVIN COOKE *

The Woodhead electrics

The trans-Pennine Woodhead route was intended to herald a dazzling post-steam era for British Railways when it was electrified in 1954.

However, within three decades its passenger services were withdrawn after British Railways came to regard it as a huge white elephant, and today it is no more, despite regular calls for it to be reopened.

The Sheffield, Ashton-under-Lyne & Manchester Railway opened the line in 1845 after it had been engineered by Joseph Locke. Its original eastern terminus was at Bridgehouses station, but after the company had become part of the Manchester, Sheffield & Lincolnshire Railway, a two-thirds-of-a-mile extension to the new Sheffield Victoria station opened in 1851. Its early success led to heavy passenger and freight traffic and sections were made four track.

Faced with the problem of operating heavy coal trains on the steep Wath - Penistone section, the Great Central Railway came up with the idea of electrifying the route, despite the fact that electric traction then was still in its infancy.

It was the LNER that drew up concrete electrification plans in 1936 and began installing gantries for the overhead wires. At Doncaster works, LNER chief mechanical engineer, Sir Nigel Gresley, produced the prototype electric locomotive for the route in 1941, LNER Bo-Bo No. 6701, but the project stalled because of the Second World War. In

1947, it was loaned to Dutch Railways to help with a postwar shortage of locomotives, and was given the nickname 'Tommy'.

The plans for the route were revived after the war, and included building a new double-track Woodhead Tunnel to replace the Victorian single-bore originals, and in September 1954 the first electric services were running. It was promoted in a blaze of publicity as Britain's first all-electric main line.

Manchester-Sheffield-Wath was finally electrified throughout in 1955 using a 1500v DC system, which is standard in the Netherlands. However, the comparatively low voltage necessitated a large number of electricity substations and heavy cabling, and advances in technology eventually saw the UK network adopt the 25kV overhead system as standard. As a result, the Woodhead route remained as a one-off.

Two types of electric locomotives were built for the route: the prototype became the first of 58 locomotives, the production batch all being built at Gorton. They were classified EM1, later Class 76, and were initially intended primarily for freight trains.

They were followed by the larger EM2 Co-Cos or Class 77s, also built at Gorton and primarily used for express passenger trains between Manchester Piccadilly and Sheffield Victoria.

Also Class 506 electric multiple units were built for suburban services between Manchester, Glossop and Hadfield. A depot at Reddish was

built in 1954 to maintain the electric stock.

The route from Manchester to Sheffield was 41½ miles with stations at Manchester, Gorton, Guide Bridge, Newton, Godley Junction, Mottram, Glossop and Dinting, Glossop Central, Hadfield, Crowden, Woodhead, Dunford Bridge, Hazlehead Bridge, Penistone, Wortley, Deepcar, Oughtibridge, Wadsley Bridge, Neepsend and Sheffield.

However, despite major investment, the line would not survive the Beeching cuts.

British Railways chairman Dr Richard Beeching's report of 1963 called for the eradication of routes which "doubled up", and he recommended that the one Manchester-Sheffield line to remain open to passengers should be Woodhead. Despite closing the intermediate stations in 1964, he saw the Woodhead route as the way forward.

However, other factors came into play, which meant that the Hope Valley line through Edale was saved instead after locals objected strongly and convincingly to its closure. Sheffield Victoria station was earmarked for closure, but British Railways would have then been faced with the high cost of electrifying a route into Sheffield Midland. Also, the opening of the giant Fiddlers Ferry Power Station near Widnes was on the horizon, necessitating more trans-Pennine freight train paths from the South Yorkshire Coalfield, without having to switch from electric to diesel haulage for part of the journey.

In September 1969, all of the Class 77s were bought by the Dutch national railway operator Nederlandse Spoorwegen and became Class NS 1500. Six remained in service until 1986.

Passenger services on the Woodhead route were then delegated to the Class 76s, but the trans-Pennine route closed to passengers on January 5, 1970. A local electric service remained at the Manchester end while the Sheffield-Penistone service was switched to diesel haulage.

Woodhead remained open for freight, but the Seventies saw a downturn in coal traffic across the Pennines. The electric locomotives and apparatus needed renewing, a prospect that found no sympathy with British Rail which had always done its best to eradicate nonstandard components of the network wherever possible.

The final freight train ran on July 17, 1981. As the route became mothballed, there were calls for it to be reopened, but the tracks over the Pennines were lifted in the mid-Eighties.

The suburban passenger service between Manchester, Glossop and Hadfield was converted to 25kV AC overhead in December 1984, with the Class 506 EMUs withdrawn and replaced by Class 303 EMUs from Glasgow. Services are now operated by Class 323 EMUs.

The trackbed between Hadfield and Woodhead Tunnel is now the Longdendale Trail for hikers and cyclists. The three tunnels at Woodhead are owned by National Grid, which in 2008 decided to relocate its electricity cables from the Victorian to the 1953 tunnel, meaning that it could not be reused for rail traffic.

The single line from Woodburn Junction on the Sheffield to Lincoln Line to Deepcar remains open to serve the Tata steelworks at Stocksbridge in midweek.

Yet the idea of reopening the whole route did not go away, and probably never will. In 1999 Central Railway proposed using it as part of a new scheme to connect Liverpool to London.

In 2002 the Transpennine Rail Group produced evidence to a transport select committee which identified interest from bidders for the Transpennine rail franchise in reopening the Woodhead route. In 2006, Translink proposed to rebuild the route for freight.

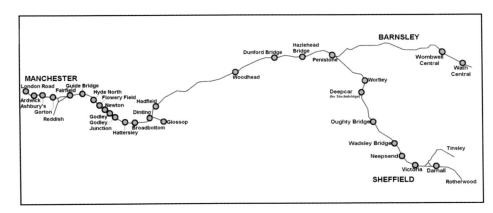

A group operating under the banner of the Don Valley Railway wants to rebuild the route from Deepcar to Sheffield as a double-tracked heritage line to link up with the Sheffield Supertram at Nunnery Junction. Also, Sheffield City Council and South Yorkshire Passenger Transport Executive have been investigating the possibility of restarting passenger services between Sheffield and Stocksbridge.

The route plays its part on the Great Central preservation story. All but one of the Class 76s were scrapped after the route closed, the exception being No. 26020 (76020) which was built with stainless-steel handrails and had

been exhibited at the Festival of Britain in 1951, later pulling the opening day train through the Woodhead Tunnel. It is now a static exhibit inside the Great Hall of the National Railway Museum in York. A cabside from No. 76039 *Hector* and a door from No. 76051 are preserved at Barrow Hill Roundhouse.

Three Class 77s survive: No. 27000 *Electra* (Dutch 1502) at the Midland Railway - Butterley, No. 27001 *Ariadne* (1505) in the Museum of Science and Industry in Manchester and No. 27003 *Diana* (1501), which has been preserved in the Netherlands by Werkgroep 1501. ∎

Still carrying its Dutch livery, reimported Class 77 No. 27001 *Ariadne* in the Museum of Science and Industry in Manchester. MOSI

The sole-surviving Class 76, No. 26020, inside the National Railway Museum at York. ROBIN JONES

Reimported Class 77 No. 27000 *Electra* inside the Midland Railway-Butterley. ROBIN JONES

CHAPTER 7

Buckinghamshire Railway Centre

Poster from 1899, inside the museum building, highlighting Quainton Road's Great Central heritage. ROBIN JONES

The year before the Main Line Preservation Group obtained its lease on Loughborough station, part of the Great Central Railway's main line to London had been revived as a preservation base, in what evolved into the Buckinghamshire Railway Centre.

Quainton Road station, which lies 44 miles from London, dates back to 1868, following the opening of the Aylesbury & Buckingham Railway on September 23 that year.

The 3rd Duke of Buckingham, Richard Plantagenet Campbell Temple-Nugent-Brydges-Chandos-Grenville, at one time chairman of the LNWR, pressurised the railway to follow a route near his home at Wotton House and to open a station at the nearest point to it.

Serving a relatively unpopulated and very rural area, Quainton Road was little more than a basic station at that time. Two years later, standard gauge and initially horse-drawn

Wotton Tramway was built to link the Wotton estate to the railway, carrying agricultural produce and building materials. When the line was extended to the village of Brill, it was relaid for use by steam locomotives and became known as the Brill Tramway.

All goods to and from the Brill Tramway passed through Quainton Road, making it relatively heavily used despite its geographical isolation. Traffic increased further when construction began on Ferdinand de Rothschild's mansion, Waddesdon Manor. The MP was also a banker, art collector, and High Sherriff of Buckinghamshire.

In the 1880s, it was proposed to extend the Brill Tramway to Oxford, which would have turned Quainton Road into a major junction, but the plans were abandoned, partly due to the high cost of tunnelling. The Great Central Railway's London Extension arrived in 1899.

Buckinghamshire Railway Centre flagship locomotive Metropolitan Railway 'E' class 0-4-4T No. 1 at the Quainton Road water tower on February 17, 2013.

No. 1 is the sole survivor of a class of seven engines designed for use on the Baker Street to Verney Junction service. Built in 1898, it was the last locomotive constructed at Neasden Works. For more than two decades, these locos were the mainstay of Metropolitan services to Aylesbury, after being displaced from the inner London lines through electrification.

When the Metropolitan Railway was taken over by the London Passenger Transport Board on April 13, 1933, No. 1 became London Transport No. L44. After the Second World War, it and sisters Nos. L46 and L478 frequently worked Baker Street to Aylesbury services, and may have run as far as Quainton Road.

As L44, No. 1 hauled the last steam train on the Chesham branch in July 1960 and the last steam-hauled passenger train anywhere on the Underground system in 1961. It was finally withdrawn after taking part in the Metropolitan Centenary parade at Neasden on May 23, 1963.

Following withdrawal, No. L44 was bought by the London Railway Preservation Society and the Met Tank Appeal Fund. It was delivered in steam onto the LRPS's temporary store at Skimpot Lane, Luton on March 26, 1964, and finally arrived at Quainton Road on September 23, 1970, after being stored at Aylesbury for two years.

Following its overhaul at Quainton, No. 1 was maintained to the standard required of British Rail main line running, and in addition to running at the centre, also headed occasional specials organised by London Underground.

After its previous boiler ticket expired in October 2010, agreement was reached with London Transport Museum for No. 1 to again be overhauled at Bill Parker's Flour Mill workshop at Bream, in the Forest of Dean, prior to a series of runs over the Underground to mark the 150th anniversary in 2013 of the system's first line, the Metropolitan Railway.

The trips proved to be a dazzling success and earned the museum and London Underground the Heritage Railway Association's top accolade, the 2013 Peter Manisty Award for Excellence.

In February that year, No. 1 returned home to Quainton Road where it was paired with Metropolitan Railway Dreadnought Carriage No. 465 (on extended loan from the Vintage Carriages Trust), based at Ingrow on the Keighley & Worth Valley Railway.

It also starred in the special runs over the Underground in August 2014 to mark the 150th anniversary of the Hammersmith & City Line and also the 125th anniversary of the Chesham branch. ROBIN JONES

The immaculately restored Quainton Road main station building, built to serve the Great Central Railway's London Extension. ROBIN JONES

Parallel running: 1874-built LSWR Beattie well tank No. 30585 and industrial Peckett 0-4-0ST No. 2087 of 1948 *Gibraltar* in action on the Buckinghamshire Railway Centre running lines on October 8, 2006. No. 30585 was one of two 2-4-0WTs which entered preservation after withdrawal from the Wenfordbridge mineral branch at Bodmin, where they had worked for six decades after being declared obsolete elsewhere. It was bought from British Railways in 1964 by the London Railway Preservation Society and stored at Bishops Stortford until 1969. No. 2087 was supplied new to Courtaulds and entered preservation following withdrawal in 1968. ROBIN JONES

Two trains in operation along part of the London Extension: Metropolitan Railway E class 0-4-4T No. 1 heading a passenger train on Buckinghamshire Railway Centre's eastern sidings running line, passing a service on the Vale of Aylesbury Model Engineering Society's kilometre-long, multi-gauge running line, which shares the venue, on February 17, 2013. ROBIN JONES

The first open day at Quainton Road was held in August 1969, with Hudswell Clarke 0-6-0T No. 1334 of 1918 *Sir Thomas* on the train, with Hunslet 0-6-0ST No. 3850 of 1958 *Juno* waiting to take over. BRC

The GCR built the existing brick station in a joint venture with the Metropolitan Railway, which had absorbed the Aylesbury & Buckingham Railway, and also took over the Brill Tramway that year.

It was then that Quainton Road became a significant junction at which trains from four directions met, and became by far the busiest of the Metropolitan Railway's rural stations.

The London Transport Passenger Board was formed in 1933, taking over the Metropolitan Railway and closing the Brill Tramway in 1935. From 1936, London Underground services were withdrawn north of Aylesbury, leaving the LNER, as successor to the GCR, the only operator using the station, although Underground services were restored for a short period in the 1940s.

Quainton Road closed to passengers on March 4, 1963, and to goods on July 4, 1966. The GCR route from Aylesbury to Rugby was abandoned on September 3 that year, leaving just the GCR line from Aylesbury to Calvert on the Oxford to Bletchley line open for freight, which used a spur line, installed in 1942 at Calvert Junction. The line was singled shortly afterwards, and the signalbox at Quainton Road was abandoned on August 13, 1967, when the points connecting to the goods yard were disconnected.

Meanwhile, the London Railway Preservation Society was founded in 1962 to preserve artefacts representing the capital's railway heritage. It bought a series of former London Underground vehicles and collectables and built up the largest collection of LNWR memorabilia.

The items were at first temporarily stored at depots in Luton and Bishop's Stortford, but as

March 2, 1963, was the last day of passenger services to Quainton Road under British Railways. Calling is a DMU, working an Aylesbury to Brackley local. BRC

Brill Tramway began at Quainton Road, and plans in the late 19th century to extend it to Oxford came to nothing, but in the early 21st century, Oxford came to Quainton Road! The Buckinghamshire Railway Centre is now home to the university city's magnificent LNWR Rewley Road terminus. ROBIN JONES

Tyseley Locomotive Works' GWR Castle 4-6-0 No. 5080 *Defiant*, on loan to the Buckinghamshire Railway Centre, is seen on static display inside the Rewley Road station building. ROBIN JONES

The unique wooden waiting room on the Brill branch platform now houses exhibits from the former tramway. ROBIN JONES

space became short, the society began to search for a permanent home, looking at several sites before choosing Quainton Road station.

The Quainton Railway Society Ltd was formed in 1969 and the LRPS was formally incorporated into it on April 24, 1971. The society was granted charitable status the following year, and became known as the Buckinghamshire Railway Centre.

As the station did not have any covered accommodation when the society first moved to the site, a building was erected in the down yard, which spanned 150ft-long tracks, incorporating workshops, a museum and refreshments facility.

The station became a bookshop and ticket office, while the extensive sidings (disconnected from the main line in 1967) were used for locomotive restoration. The society eventually restored the main station building to its 1900 appearance.

Another building was acquired from London Transport and was relocated to Quainton from Wembley Park station. It became known as the Wembley Shed and houses engines and carriages awaiting restoration. A 60ft turntable was also later installed.

There are no regular passenger train services, but rides are offered along two running lines in the yards either side of the working Network Rail line, which runs through the middle of the centre. The NR line is regularly used by landfill trains running from waste transfer depots in Greater London to the

Great Central it ain't: Aveling & Porter flywheel-driven 0-4-0 No. 807, seen on static display inside the Quainton Road museum building, was one of a pair which worked on the Wotton Tramway, later known as the Brill branch. Supplied in January 1872, it had a maximum speed of 4mph. Both were withdrawn in 1894 and replaced by two Manning Wardle K-Class saddle tanks. No. 807 then worked at the Nether Heyford Brickworks in Northamptonshire, which closed in 1940. After being bought by the Industrial Locomotive Society, in 1951 London Transport agreed to store it at Neasden Depot. In 1957 it was officially handed over to the British Transport Commission for display at the former Museum of British Transport, Clapham, and in 1980 arrived at the London Transport Museum in Covent Garden. ROBIN JONES

Former Kent cement line Barclay 0-4-0ST No. 699 of 1891 *Swanscombe* arrived at Quainton Road on April 18, 1969, and in 1975 became a TV celebrity when it steamed on the BBC children's programme Play School. ROBIN JONES

former brick pits at Calvert. The main station building is on the up side of the NR line with a smaller wooden building on the platform between the currently vacant down line trackbed and the platform from which the Brill branch ran. Services operate from Aylesbury to Quainton Road station when the centre holds special events. They started in 1988, when Chiltern Railways laid on Saturday Christmas shopping services between Aylesbury and Bletchley.

An adjacent Second World War Ministry of Food buffer depot has been taken over to display many items awaiting their turn in the restoration queue. The centre also has a members' reference library and storerooms maintained to the exacting standards of an accredited museum. With buildings dating from

1874 to the 1960s most major developments in railway history can be viewed.

The museum has also acquired the LNWR's Oxford Rewley Road terminus station building, which closed to passengers on October 1, 1951. Trains were diverted to the current Oxford station.

Rewley Road – a sister building to the Crystal Palace, which was built from similar components – was dismantled in 1999, in co-operation with London's Science Museum. The main station building and part of the platform canopy were then moved to BRC and re-erected in 2002 at Quainton Road, providing a museum display building, cafe and society offices.

Today, Quainton Road is considered to be one of the best-preserved period railway stations in England and is regularly used as a

filming location for period drama. The Jewel in the Crown, Black Orchid (the fifth serial of the 19th Doctor Who season) and Midsomer Murders have been filmed there.

The Buckinghamshire Railway Centre has for some years been talking to Network Rail about relinking its sidings to the main line so it can run services to Aylesbury when the line is not in use by freight trains.

Officials have also considered a scheme to rebuild part of the Brill Tramway between Quainton Road and Waddesdon Road. However, Quainton Road may soon find itself if not on, then next to High Speed 2, the next major rail route between London and the north.

The proposed route passes immediately to the west of the centre, and would permanently sever the route of the tramway. ∎

Early Quainton Road preservation pioneer: Hunslet 0-6-0ST No. 3850 of 1958 *Juno* in steam at an open day in 1971. Built in 1958 for Stewarts & Lloyds of Buckminster in Rutland, it worked in ironstone quarries until 1968. It was then bought by the Ivatt Trust, which donated it to the Isle of Wight Steam Railway in 2009. It is currently on loan to the National Railway Museum's Locomotion museum at Shildon. BRC

GWR 0-6-0PT No. 7715 (its latter-day working life incarnation at London Underground was L99) at work at Quainton Road in 1970. Thirteen 57xxs were bought by London Transport between 1956-63 for use on the London Underground network, hauling freight and permanent way trains, the last remaining in use until 1971. L99 was bought in working order from London Transport in 1969. BRC

Metropolitan Railway No. 1 heads back to base on the western running line at Quainton Road. ROBIN JONES

LMS Jubilee No. 5596 *Bahamas* at Dinting Railway Centre on June 20, 1976. BRIAN SHARPE

Dinting:
the lost railway museum

In 1966, the Stockport (Bahamas) Locomotive Society was formed, with the aim of saving LMS Jubilee 4-6-0 No. 45596 *Bahamas* from ending up in a scrapyard.

Withdrawn from service in July 1966, and left at the back of Stockport Edgeley shed where it had been allocated four years previously, *Bahamas* was finally bought for £6000, just as preparations were being made to cut it up for scrap.

Repainted in LMS crimson lake livery, and having just been overhauled by Hunslet in Leeds, it was formally handed over to society officials in March 1968.

It then steamed back over the Pennines to Edgeley depot where it was displayed with A3 Pacific No. 4472 *Flying Scotsman* and BR

Britannia Pacific No. 70013 *Oliver Cromwell*.

In late 1968, the society concluded a lease on the engine shed at Dinting station near Glossop, and moved *Bahamas* there from Bury, where it had been housed for several months.

The Sheffield, Ashton-under-Lyne & Manchester Railway opened a station called Glossop in 1842, but it was renamed when the Glossop branch opened in 1845. In 1847, a temporary Glossop Junction station was built, on the site of which the present Dinting station was built a year later, mainly serving the population of Gamesley.

The SAMR later became part of the Manchester, Sheffield & Lincolnshire Railway, which in 1894 erected the brick-built through-road engine shed, with a coal stage and water tank.

The LNER closed the depot in 1935 and reopened it in 1942, but British Railways closed it in 1954, leaving the engine shed still intact.

Taken over by the society, the cramped and inconvenient site with its one engine shed turned into a nine-acre major steam centre, under the banner of the Dinting Railway Centre, with a new exhibition shed being built. Southern Railway Schools 4-4-0 No. 30925 *Cheltenham* and, yes, Great Central O4 2-8-0 No. 63601 were allocated from the National Collection, and Geoff Drury's LNER Pacifics A4 No. 19 *Bittern* and No. 532 *Blue Peter*, after a period of open storage at Walton colliery near Wakefield, moved to Dinting.

LMS Royal Scot 4-6-0 No. 6115 *Scots*

Great Central history lost to preservation: Dinting engine shed today. BRIAN SHARPE

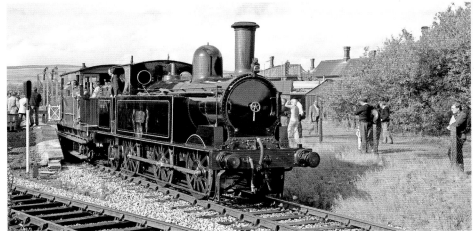
LNWR Webb 0-6-2T Coal Tank No. 1054 giving brake van rides on the demonstration line at Dinting Railway Centre on October 3, 1982. DAVID INGHAM*

LMS Stanier rebuilt Royal Scot 4-6-0 No. 6115 (46115) *Scots Guardsman* in 1946 LMS lined black livery giving brake van rides at Dinting Railway Centre in April 1980. HUGH LLEWELLYN*

Guardsman, which had been bought from British Railways by Bob Bill, was inherited by his son and daughter on his death. It arrived at Dinting Railway Centre in May 1969.

In 1978, it was returned to steam resplendent in postwar Ivatt LMS black livery. After a test run to Sheffield, No. 6115 *Scots Guardsman* made just two main line passenger outings before BR tightened its boiler regulations with which the engine no longer complied. Peter Bill, the son of the original owner and retired switchgear company director, then sold the locomotive to the 46115 Scots Guardsman Trust.

Scots Guardsman was destined not to pull another train for 30 years, until it had undergone a rebuild by the West Coast Railway Company at Carnforth, and is now a regular main line performer.

At Dinting, the society acquired steam engineering expertise, operating locomotives such as LMS Jubilee No. 5690 *Leander* and overhauling LNWR 0-6-2 Coal Tank No. 1054 as well as maintaining *Bahamas*. Also on display was Woodhead route veteran EM1 Bo-Bo No. 26020.

The Buxton Model Engineering Society built a miniature railway at Dinting in 1976.

A dispute over the lease following a financial crisis led to the Bahamas Society being evicted from Dinting in 1990, and the centre closed.

A sad loss to the heritage sector indeed, but the society found a new welcome home at Ingrow station on the Keighley & Worth Valley Railway, where it restored an 1867-built Midland Railway warehouse as the Ingrow Loco Museum & Workshop.

On September 20, 2010, the former Dinting Railway Centre site was sold at auction for £150,000, despite a guide price of a mere £25,000. Outbid was the Dinting Railway Trust, a volunteer group that had hoped to buy it and restart the steam centre, which for so long had been a household name in preservation circles.

At the time of writing, Dinting's engine shed was still standing, but the site was largely reclaimed by nature as the owners postulate about its future. A housing estate, perhaps?

Either way, the centre's fortunes have been the opposite of those of the Buckinghamshire Railway Centre. ∎

CHAPTER 9

The second coming

MAIN PICTURE: Hauling its first train in preservation, BR Standard 8P Pacific No. 71000 *Duke of Gloucester* departs from Rothley on October 3, 1986. BRIAN SHARPE

In the early days of the GCR, Hunslet 0-6-0ST *Robert Nelson No. 4* (1800 of 1936) approaches Quorn & Woodhouse. BRIAN SHARPE

The closure of the Great Central went ahead in 1969, despite mass public protests.

Groups who opposed the axing of the route came together for a meeting in a waiting room at Leicester Central, and the Main Line Preservation Group was formed in January that year.

The revivalists' original plan was the restoration of the whole line from Arkwright Street to Rugby Central, but like many other similar schemes, this aim was revised down, owing to time and financial constraints, to the Loughborough-Nottingham section, chosen because of its scenery and comparatively few major engineering works.

The group sought to follow the blueprint of other successful revival schemes, such as the Bluebell, Dart Valley and Keighley & Worth Valley railways. The revivalists could not restore public timetabled services, but they could create a linear museum on which steam trains could be operated as a tourist attraction over a section of line.

However, what was markedly different about this scheme from the outset was that the group wanted to save a double-track section of line, for main line locomotives representing the 'Big Four' companies and British Railways to one day again haul appropriate trains in an authentic setting.

In April 1969, the group's land agent surveyed the line, and after British Rail pulled out of Loughborough Central in May, separate groups were formed to prevent vandalism.

In September, talks were opened with British Rail London Midland Estates about possibly buying the line.

In the meantime, Loughborough County Council had been considering a scheme to convert a section of the line into a road between the A6 and A60.

The asking price for the line was £383,000, for the land between Loughborough and Birstall together with the double track between Loughborough and Quorn, and a single track between Quorn and Belgrave & Birstall.

However, an appeal raised only £50,000, and British Rail added an extra £1000 a month interest to hold off lifting the track.

Local landowner Lord Lanesborough, through whose estate the railway ran, became president of the group, which embarked on a series of exhibitions and film shows to publicise its aims.

January 1970 saw the top floor of Loughborough Central leased, with renovation beginning, and two months later, an offer to buy the line was made to British Rail.

That summer, the Main Line Preservation Group began talks to locomotive owners while making an application for a Light Railway Order giving it statutory powers to run the line.

In January 1971, a new company formed to run the revived section of line; Main Line Steam Trust Ltd, received charitable status. HM Railway Inspectorate visited and found the state of the line to be good and gave broad approval for the scheme.

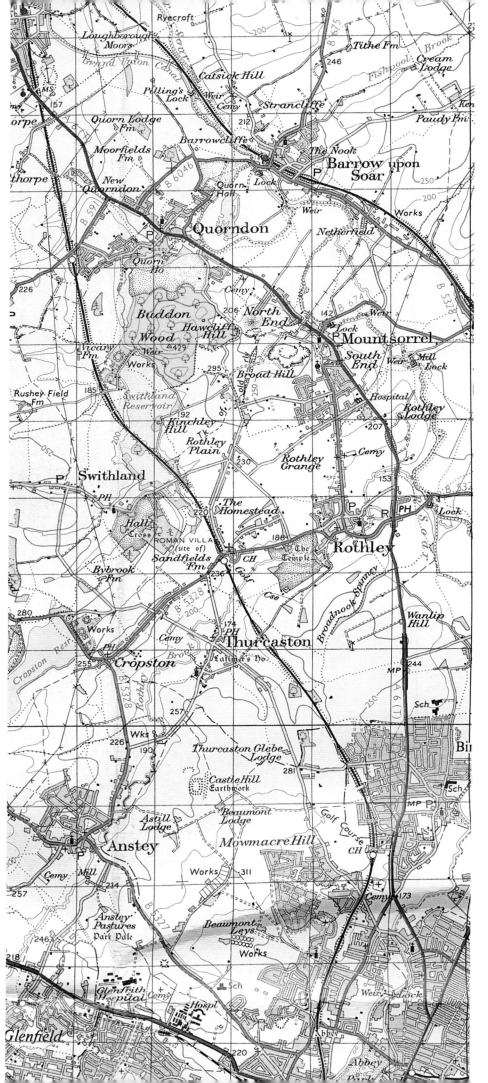

Two months later, Leicester County Council finally abandoned the idea of building a road on the trackbed, removing a major doubt about the viability of the revival scheme.

Fundraising began that summer, and in September, the trust formally took over from the preservation group.

Meanwhile, British Rail retained a single track from Loughborough to Ruddington to access the Ministry of Defence base there, as well as British Gypsum freight to Hotchley Hill. The revivalists had the ultimate aim of running from Ruddington in the north to Belgrave & Birstall in the south, a distance of 18 miles.

THE FIRST GREEN SHOOTS

In January 1973, Loughborough Central was reopened to the public, and footplate rides within the station limits were offered.

On September 30, 1973, history was made when the first public train ran from Loughborough to Quorn & Woodhouse, under British Rail supervision, as no Light Railway Order had yet been granted. Proudly heading the train was LMS 'Black Five' 4-6-0 No. 5231. Before then, a reopening special had been run on July 24, comprising Swedish-built Norwegian State Railways 2-6-0 No. 377 *King Haakon VII* hauling a single coach. This locomotive, wholly historically non-authentic for a Great Central line, had been bought for preservation in 1969 and imported into the UK, being first based at Loughborough.

Initial services were operated by engines on the front and back of the train comprising two coaches, because there were no run-round facilities at Quorn & Woodhouse at that time. It was decided to build a large locomotive shed to the north of Loughborough Central, but care was taken to leave a way through for a possible future extension to Ruddington. At the same time, British Rail lifted the track beyond Loughborough, as the Ruddington branch would from then on be connected directly to the Midland Main Line by a new chord.

Regular operation of services between Loughborough and Quorn & Woodhouse was achieved by July 1974. At that time the double track from Loughborough Central to Quorn & Woodhouse and the single line south to Thurmaston Road bridge in Leicester was still in situ, before the building of the A563 ring road, which severed the line south of Birstall.

A trial weekend in September 1975 saw trains run into Rothley for the first time, the first being a VIP special again hauled by *King Haakon VII*.

The Great Central Railway Company (1976) Limited was incorporated as a private company on May 6 that year, and a public company three days later, when No. 5231 was named *3rd Volunteer Battalion, The Worcestershire and Sherwood Foresters Regiment* at Quorn. It was reputed to be the longest name ever given to a locomotive, but is no longer carried by this engine. At this time trains were still being operated under BR supervision.

LEFT: The Loughborough to Leicester section of the Great Central Railway main line, as depicted on an Ordnance Survey One Inch map of 1962.

Early remedial work to the Loughborough Central platform canopy carried out after the revivalists moved in. GCR

The July 24, 1973 reopening special to Quorn & Woodhouse headed by *King Haakon VII* taking on water at Loughborough. GCR

The Quorn & Woodhouse reopening special arrives at its destination. GCR

A Loughborough open day with traction engines and house organ providing entertainment at the north end of the platform on April 13, 1974. DENNIS WILCOCK/GCR

At the time, the Main Line Steam Trust was still struggling to find the purchase price and had to continue paying the monthly interest. In December 1975, British Rail gave the trust an ultimatum to buy the track outright by April 1, or it would be lifted.

A share issue was launched to buy the track from BR, but initially it was possibly to buy only a single-track section from Loughborough to Quorn. However, with the help of the Main Line Steam Trust and a substantial bank loan, the company bought the single line between Quorn and Rothley, giving a total of five route miles. British Railways then lifted the remainder of the track, the second track between Loughborough and Quorn, and the Rothley to Birstall section. The Great Central was forced to close in July and August 1976, its peak season, while the second line between Loughborough and Quorn was lifted.

It seemed that the possibility of saving a stretch of double track had come to an end.

THE EARLY LOCOMOTIVE FLEET

Most of the early services were handled by *King Haakon VII*, Hunslet 0-6-0ST No. 1800 of 1936 *Robert Nelson No.4*, (now at the private Riverstown Old Corn Mill Railway in Ireland), Manning Wardle 0-6-0ST *Littleton No. 5* No. 2018 of 1922 (now at the Avon Valley Railway), Robert Stephenson & Hawthorns 0-6-0ST No. 6947, which had been converted by

Humble beginnings: footplate and brakevan rides for 5p a time were offered at Loughborough station behind Robert Stephenson & Hawthorns 0-6-0T No. 39, from June 21-24, 1973. GCR

LMS 'Black Five' 4-6-0 No. 5231 departs from Loughborough on Sunday, June 20, 1976, before the second track was lifted by British Rail.
BRIAN SHARPE

members from a saddle tank to a side tank (now with the Darlington Railway Preservation Society), Hawthorn Leslie 0-4-0ST No. 3581 of 1924 *Marston, Thompson & Evershed No. 3* (now at the Foxfield Railway), and No. 5231.

It was very much a 'starter' line, using whatever locomotives were available and economical to run, rather than fulfilling a main line mission statement.

However, the extension of the line to Rothley encouraged more locomotive owners to base their engines there. The Witherslack Hall Society moved its Western Region 4-6-0 No. 6990 *Witherslack Hall* there from Barry scrapyard in December 1975.

Witherslack Hall was a veteran of the route, for it had run along the London Extension during the locomotive exchanges of 1948, in which different 'Big Four' locomotives were trialled over different regions of the newly nationalised railway. During the trials, *Witherslack Hall* competed against a LNER B1, a Southern Railway Bulleid West Country light Pacific and a LMS 'Black Five'. Modified Halls also regularly worked over the Great Central main line while running over the Banbury to Woodford Halse link.

While the railway was closed in the summer of 1976, a much-needed run-round loop was installed at Loughborough Central, eliminating time-consuming and expensive shunting procedures.

The trust was still working flat out to buy the track between Rothley and Quorn for £70,000. Rothley station was refitted with gas lighting, with the apparatus having been brought from British Rail's Collector's Corner in London. The lighting was switched on by Sir Mark Henig, chairman of the English Tourist Board, during the Bonfire Night celebrations on November 5.

THE FUTURE SECURED

In 1977, British Rail gave the railway an ultimatum to hand over the purchase price of the line by January 20, or the line between Quorn and Rothley would be lifted. Two interest-free loans were obtained from Leicestershire businessmen and topped up by a bank loan, and the money was handed over with only a day to spare.

With a far-sighted vision sadly absent from many other local authorities of the day, Charnwood Borough Council agreed to purchase the land and buildings of the whole route from Loughborough to Belgrave & Birstall, where the vandal-damaged original station was demolished the following year.

No. 377, now a static exhibit at Bressingham Steam Museum, was involved in a serious accident at Woodthorpe bridge on March 7, 1976, when a badly fitted fusible plug blew out of the crown plate of the firebox leaving a hole from which a high-velocity jet of steam and water escaped. There were no casualties among the 200 passengers on the five-coach train but two out of four people on the footplate, Robert Anderson and Michael Mountford, received painful burns and required hospital treatment.

Hunslet 0-6-0ST No. 1800 of 1936 *Robert Nelson No. 4* heads a GCR Marylebone Extension 75th anniversary special on March 23, 1974. Already there is a restaurant car in the train: the revived GCR was to become famous for its dining services. GRAHAM WIGNALL/GCR

The Great Central Railway Company (1976) Limited was incorporated as a public company on May 9, 1976, when LMS 'Black Five' No. 5231 was named *3rd Volunteer Battalion, The Worcestershire and Sherwood Foresters Regiment* at Quorn & Woodhouse. GCR

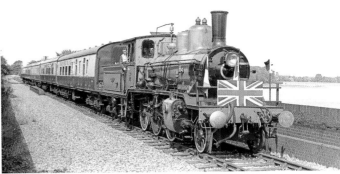

September 6, 1975, saw heritage-era trains run into Rothley for the first time, the first being a VIP special hauled by Swedish-built Norwegian State Railways 2-6-0 No. 377 *King Haakon VII*, seen crossing Swithland viaduct. GCR

In 1977, two GCR directors bought LMS Jubilee 4-6-0 No. 5690 *Leander*, as a crucial step in fulfilling the original aim of running big main line locomotives on a main line railway. *Leander* had run over the route in 1962.

In April 1978, Charnwood Borough Council and the railway agreed a 99-year lease on the land and buildings, allowing the line to operate with the cost of the lease £1750 a year.

That year, the company and the council were jointly awarded a Light Railway Order which came into effect on March 31, the day the GCR finally took complete control of all train operations. From then on, BR no longer needed to supervise operations, but at least one of the supervisors became a volunteer on the line.

Also in 1978, LNER-design B1 4-6-0 No. 1306 *Mayflower* (now at the North Norfolk Railway) and N2 0-6-2T No. 4744 (which starred in the EMI movie The Railway Children pulling the 'Scotch Express' while based on the Keighley & Worth Valley Railway) arrived and formed the mainstay of motive power the following year, during which a second Gresley teak buffet coach and four Mk.1 carriages from the Nene Valley Railway arrived.

As with so many of our top heritage lines, the GCR had relied on industrial types in those formative years, but by now it was beginning to look more and more like a steam-era main line.

In 1979, *Mayflower* ran service for 109 days: by this time the modern-day GCR was already running eight-coach trains so remarkable had been its progress during the first decade.

Norwegian State Railways 2-6-0 No. 377 *King Haakon VII* inside Loughborough shed facing original GCR Director class 4-4-0 No. 506 *Butler Henderson*, at that time a static exhibit. GRAHAM WIGNALL/GCR

RSH 0-6-0ST No. 39 (6988), converted to a side tank in GCR livery, is seen at Loughborough on May 27, 1979. Industrial types were still in service on the line at this time. BRIAN SHARPE

The Duke of Gloucester inspects progress on No. 71000 *Duke of Gloucester* before setting off on a special train to inaugurate the Leicester North extension on July 8, 1985. And the Rothley special train crosses Swithland viaduct. DENNIS WILCOCK/GCR

Ours at last: GCR directors and borough council representatives pictured in April 1978, after signing a 99-year lease on the land and buildings, allowing the line to operate. In the centre holding the lease is Bill Ford who had championed the joint venture to save the line between the council and the railway. BILL SQUIRES/GCR

In a scene now utterly transformed, LNER B1 4-6-0 No. 1306 *Mayflower* and GNR N2 0-6-2 No. 4744 depart from Loughborough Central on the Great Central Railway on May 27, 1979. BRIAN SHARPE

THE BIGGEST SETBACK OF ALL

That winter, one of the biggest obstacles to reopening all the way from the southern edge of Nottingham to the fringe of Leicester appeared. The Great Central bridge over the Midland Main Line along with the southern embankment leading to it had been demolished.

Its absence has not deterred revivalists who dream of creating the world's first inter-city heritage railway, but endless discussions have taken place over the ensuing years as to how to replace it.

A will-o'-the-wisp, every time a costing was produced, it was always outside the grasp of the railway's finances or those of potential grant-funding bodies. In time, the missing bridge came to be regarded as the biggest obstacle in the entire British preservation portfolio.

If only more had been done to save it back then…

LNER B1 4-6-0 No. 1306 *Mayflower* departs from Quorn on the Great Central Railway on February 1, 1981. BRIAN SHARPE

The Duke of Gloucester inserts a golden spike into the start of the Leicester North extension on July 1985. DENNIS WILCOCK/GCR

Early tracklaying being carried out on the extension to Leicester North. DENNIS WILCOCK/GCR

GNR Stirling Single No. 1 passes Swithland on December 6, 1981. BRIAN SHARPE

MORE ENGINES ARRIVE

In 1980, the railway's first general manager, D Grahame Handley, was appointed. The following year, the line was graced by a three-month visit from one of Britain's most famous steam locomotives in Great Northern Railway Stirling single 4-2-2 No. 1, courtesy of the NRM.

The 1907-built engine's restoration to working order had been sponsored by a West German and the GCR was selected for its running-in trials before a visit to Germany.

Many more locomotives would be brought to the railway for similar trials in the decades to come.

Another big landmark was passed in 1982 when one of two surviving original GCR locomotives, 11F 4-4-0 No. 506 *Butler-Henderson*, made its debut on March 27.

That year also saw the arrival of the line's first heritage-era main line diesels, Swindon-built Western Region diesel hydraulics Class 14s Nos. D9516 and D9523, acquired from British Steel at Corby where they had spent their years in industrial service following withdrawal by British Rail.

However, the railway was beset by a steam shortage in 1984, when unexpected repair problems left several locomotives out of service. The Kent & East Sussex Railway loaned Hunslet Austerity 0-6-0ST No. 25 for four months.

At the same time, the last BR train to Ruddington, 'The Ruddington Requiem' charter, ran on June 9.

Easter 1984 saw preparatory work on the installation of a passing loop at Quorn & Woodhouse begin. The immediate benefits were obvious: extra trains such as demonstration freights could be run on high days and holidays, without disrupting timetabled services.

May 1984 saw the introduction of a new timetable, which facilitated the operation of two trainsets on a regular basis, making it possible to run services every 50 minutes rather than 70. As soon as a train had arrived at Loughborough, another would be ready to leave.

PUSHING BACK TOWARDS LEICESTER

The Duke of Gloucester launched an appeal for a southern extension to Belgrave & Birstall during a visit on July 8, 1985. With the help of a substantial borough council grant, work commenced with clearance and tracklaying south from Rothley.

In 1985, GWR 2-8-0T No. 5224, now owned by Pete Waterman, entered service after becoming the line's first to be fully restored from Barry scrapyard condition, and relieving the locomotive shortage in the process.

New in traffic in 1986 were restored Barry wreck WR 4-6-0 No. 6990 *Witherslack Hall* and J94-type Austerity 0-6-0ST No. 68009, which was later sold to the North Norfolk Railway as the GCR intensified its pure main line image. Unique BR Pacific No. 71000 *Duke of Gloucester* made its first run on May 25 after a restoration programme lasting 11 years. The locomotive had been bought from Barry scrapyard with key components including the

cylinders missing, and many thought the project was 'Mission Impossible'.

With a cavalcade of locomotives, Transpo '86 was staged on September 7, highlighting the abundance of motive power now available.

At the northern end of the line, the Main Line Steam Trust appealed for money to buy the mothballed Loughborough-Ruddington line.

In 1987, the revivalists announced that following tracklaying, it was again possible to run a train from Loughborough to Belgrave & Birstall, and a members' special ran in November.

Steam also returned to the Ruddington branch, when *Robert Nelson No. 4* was loaned to British Gypsum for an open day at Rushcliffe.

The shed at Rothley was built in 1988. The following year, the company crossed a definitive watershed when it declared that it would no longer use industrial steam locomotives which were to be phased out in favour of a new 'big

A members' DMU special ran from Loughborough to Belgrave & Birstall in November 1987.

The Kent & East Sussex Railway's Hunslet Austerity 0-6-0ST No. 25, which arrived to bail the Great Central Railway out of a steam shortage, passes Woodthorpe Lane on February 24, 1985. BRIAN SHARPE

engine' policy, pursuing the aims of the original revivalists two decades before.

Meanwhile, the first stock for the planned northern extension arrived at Rushcliffe Halt.

Dame Margaret Weston officially opened the extension from Rothley to Belgrave & Birstall on November 15, 1990, giving a running line of 7½ miles. At this stage there was no passenger terminus at Belgrave & Birstall and from November 3, push-pull and DMU trains operated south of Rothley where a connection was made with the main services to Loughborough. Rothley signalbox was opened.

The GCR announced in 1990 that it intended to reinstate double track, initially from Loughborough to Rothley. Former director David Clarke agreed to provide significant financial support for the project.

Also that year, a new company, Great Central Railway (Nottingham) was formed to reopen the Ruddington branch.

July 5, 1991, saw Merchant Navy No. 35005 *Canadian Pacific* heading the 'The Great Central Limited' into the new Leicester North station, which has been built just south of the demolished Belgrave & Birstall station. The official opening was performed by Deputy Prime Minister Michael Heseltine, president of the Board of Trade.

Also in 1991, the line ran its first Christmas Day train – and has kept up the tradition ever since. It was staffed entirely by volunteers, including directors.

On February 21, 1992, *Butler-Henderson* made its final run. It then returned to the National Railway Museum York as a static exhibit, and in recent times has been on display at Barrow Hill Roundhouse near Chesterfield.

THE ASSEMBLY OF THE 'WINDCUTTER' RAKE

Thanks to an initiative by Nick Pigott, now editor of *The Railway Magazine*, an appeal was successfully launched in August 1982 to buy a rake of 16-ton 9ft wheelbase BR mineral wagons, for use in lengthy demonstration freights on the line.

More than 220,000 of these wagons, based on a Second World War design for the Ministry of War Transport, were built both in BR works and by private builders between 1950 and 1958 and they were still a regular sight on the national network in the Eighties.

In 1947 a service of regular fast freight trains was inaugurated by the LNER between marshalling yards at Annesley, near Nottingham and Woodford Halse. These trains, travelling over the Great Central route, carried coal from the Nottinghamshire coalfields and steel products from Yorkshire and the North East destined for London or South Wales. These regular services gained a reputation for fast running and the nickname of 'Windcutters', was adopted by enthusiasts, while railwaymen generally referred to them as 'Runners'. They were a regular sight on the London extension for a long time.

The appeal saw the first wagons, from Onllwyn Washery in South Wales, arrive in late August. Others came from the Rover car factory at Longbridge in Birmingham, where they had survived in use on the internal system for carrying components.

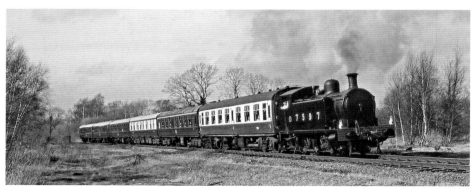

RSH 0-6-0T No. 7597 passes Swithland on March 3, 1990. BRIAN SHARPE

GWR 2-8-0T No. 5224 entered traffic in 1985 after being restored from Barry scrapyard condition. GRAHAM WIGNALL/GCR

WR 4-6-0 No. 6990 *Witherslack Hall* enters service on the GCR in 1986. GRAHAM WIGNALL/GCR

Eventually 39 mineral wagons were obtained, although three moved on to the Museum of Science and Industry in Manchester. The restoration of the mineral wagons at the GCR began in June 1993, and by 1999, 37 had been restored.

The late Patrick Whitehouse, a preservation powerhouse who had been instrumental in the formation of the Dart Valley Railway in the early Sixties, joined the GCR board in 1992, strengthening links with the Birmingham Railway Museum at Tyseley. At that time both Tyseley's LMS Jubilee No. 5593 *Kolhapur* and GWR 4-6-0 No. 7029 *Clun Castle* were based on the GCR.

The year also saw the launch of a new GCR share issue to fund the double-track project. The line was voted Independent Railway of the Year, but had already embarked on a new course which would see it elevated to even greater heights. ∎

In British Railways' livery as No. 62660, GCR Director *Butler-Henderson* passes Woodthorpe on its last run on February 22, 1992. Hopefully, it will one day return to the railway and steam again. BRIAN SHARPE

Bulleid Merchant Navy Pacific No. 35005 *Canadian Pacific* heads the 'The Great Central Limited' on July 5, 1991; the first train into the new Leicester North station, which had been built just south of the demolished Belgrave & Birstall station. JOHN EAST/GCR

CHAPTER 10

THE GREAT CENTRAL STEAM SURVIVORS

BR black-liveried GCR O4 No. 63601 approaches Kinchley Lane with a mixed freight during the winter gala on January 27, 2007. ROBIN JONES

GCR D11 4-4-0 No. 62660 *Butler-Henderson* crosses Swithland viaduct on the Great Central Railway on February 24, 1992, its last day in service. BRIAN SHARPE

At the Grouping of 1923, the Great Central's motive power stock comprised 923 tender locomotives, 435 tank engines, one petrol-electric railcar and 16 electric tramcars.

Today, just five examples of GCR/Robinson steam locomotives survive.

The first to turn on the modern-day GCR was also the first member of the GCR 11F or Improved Director 4-4-0s, No. 506 *Butler-Henderson*.

Built in 1919, it was withdrawn from use by British Railways during 1960 and preserved as part of the National Collection. It is the sole surviving GCR passenger locomotive.

At first, No. 506 was restored to static GCR condition for display at the British Transport Commission Museum at Clapham. With the

The revived Great Central celebrated its 25th anniversary in 1996. That year, original GCR 8K (O4) 2-8-0 No. 63601, which had never run in the heritage era, arrived at Quorn & Woodhouse by low-loader for restoration. JOHN EAST

became known as Improved Directors.

The most obvious modification was the use of inside admission piston valves. Side cab windows were also installed.

The newly built D11/1s were run-in at the GCR's Gorton Works and then allocated to Neasden.

The 11Fs were initially used on passenger work on the GCR system, including fast expresses from Sheffield Victoria to Marylebone. They later saw use on short distance passenger trains.

Under the LNER, the 11Fs were split into two subclasses.

D11/1s were the original GCR engines and D11/2s were those built in 1924 to a reduced loading gauge with smaller boiler mountings for hauling passenger trains on North British Railway routes in Scotland.

During the late 1940s and early 1950s, they hauled expresses between Manchester Central and Liverpool Central on the Cheshire Lines Committee routes, as well as semi-fast trains from Manchester Central via Northwich to Chester Northgate.

Their 6ft 9in driving wheels made them fast locomotives; indeed, they were considered to be Robinson's best passenger design, but were unsuitable for hauling freight trains.

Both groups of D11s were displaced by large numbers of Thompson B1 4-6-0s, and ended up in storage during the Fifties.

The 11 original 11F locos were withdrawn

during 1959-60 as diesel multiple units took over operation of the shorter distance passenger trains, and the D11/2s had gone by 1962.

FOUR O4S

Four examples of Robinson's GCR 8K 2-8-0, later LNER O4, survive. The best known is No. 63601, which was a solid performer on the heritage line for more than a decade before its boiler ticket expired.

One of the first of the class designed by Robinson to head heavy freight trains to and from the enormous new port of Immingham, No. 102 emerged from Gorton Works in January 1912.

The first 8K, No. 966, had been built in September 1911. Robinson held the opinion that the 8K was his best design.

During the First World War, the design was selected by the Railway Operating Division for large-scale production. These new locomotives as well as other examples commandeered from the GCR were known as RODs and became the standard locomotive type for service both at home and overseas.

Orders for 325 locomotives were placed in February 1917, with 196 following in 1918. After the First World War, several RODs returned to Britain and were used by some railway companies.

They were so successful that they were considered for a similar role in the Second

demise of the British Transport Commission in 1975, No. 506 entered the National Collection and was loaned to the GCR.

Restoration to running order began in 1981, and No. 506 returned to steam the following year.

It was moved to the National Railway Museum at York after its boiler certificate expired in 1992, and in 2005 was placed on long-term loan for display at Barrow Hill Engine Shed near Chesterfield, Britain's last surviving rail-connected roundhouse.

Robinson's 11E Director class, named after GCR officials, royalty and First World War battles, was so successful that five were ordered to a modified and enhanced design. They proved to be very successful, and a second batch was ordered in March 1916. They

GCR 11F 4-4-0 No. 506 *Butler-Henderson* passes Woodthorpe Lane on the Great Central Railway on November 25, 1990. BRIAN SHARPE

Contributors to the O4 appeal were invited to a special viewing of O4 No. 63601 back in steam on a murky January 28, 2000. It is seen hauling the line's Windcutter rake of mineral wagons through Swithland. The engine was unveiled to the public at a gala weekend immediately afterwards. ROBIN JONES

One of the four surviving Barnum coaches at Loughborough in 1999. HUGH LLEWELLYN

World War, but it was decided instead to produce additional examples of the LMS Stanier 8F 2-8-0.

In 1940, the GWR borrowed 30 O4s from the LNER, returning them during 1941-43.

In 1941, the military requisitioned 92 O4s for use in the Middle East, where they opened up a supply route through Persia to Russia. None returned to Britain, and were written off the LNER's books in December 1943.

It was on the LNER that they became a mainstay of freight traffic and also the most numerous of LNER heavy goods locomotives. Indeed, the O4s became one of the most successful British steam locomotive designs of the 20th century.

No. 102 was renumbered 5102 in June 1925, 3509 in April 1946, 3601 in February 1947 and finally 63601 in September 1949.

During the steam era, the locomotive was allocated to sheds serving the very arduous Pennine route from Manchester through the Woodhead Tunnel to Sheffield and on to Immingham.

Its first allocation was to Gorton on March 14, 1912, and was followed by transfers to Sheffield, Mexborough, Barnsley,

Doncaster, Frodingham near Scunthorpe and Immingham.

In addition to the heavy freight traffic to and from the docks, the locomotive was involved in the development of the steelworks at Frodingham.

Having undergone very few modifications from its original condition, it was withdrawn from service at Frodingham in June 1963.

As an example of one of the most successful steam locomotive designs ever and one of the final three O4s surviving with a Belpaire boiler, No. 63601 was chosen for preservation in 1960 as part of the National Collection.

With storage space for preserved engines then being in short supply, No. 63601 first went to Doncaster Works and then Stratford and Brighton. It then moved to Leicester where it was stored in the closed MR roundhouse but to be housed in a proposed Leicester Museum of Technology at Abbey Meadows Technology Museum.

That project having failed to take off, in 1976, No. 63601 returned to GCR metals in the form of the engine shed at Dinting Railway Centre. Locomotive department staff there decided it was restorable and No. 63601 was sent to Longsight depot to have its axlebox repaired.

In 1977, Dinting staff said that a completely new tender would be needed because the one fitted to the locomotive was vacuum and not steam braked.

In the end, the restoration carried out at Dinting was purely cosmetic. When the centre closed, No. 63601 was sent to the National Railway Museum in York.

By this time, there were many voices calling for the locomotive to be restored because of its historical importance. The Main Line Steam Trust Ltd was instrumental in bringing it to Loughborough in June 1996.

A national appeal to raise the more than £70,000 cost of restoration to full working order was launched, with the trust contributing £25,000.

An exhaustive restoration programme

entered its final stages on June 18, 1999, when the retubed boiler passed its steam test before being lowered back into the frames four days later.

Unpainted, it was displayed in light steam during the August 7-8 gala that year.

Finally, on January 24, 2000, it moved under its own steam for the first time in 36 years.

Four days later, it was coupled to the Windcutter rake of 16-ton mineral wagons and ran through Swithland Sidings for the benefit of contributors to the national appeal.

Its full public debut came the next day at the start of the winter gala weekend.

During the replacement of hundreds of copper boiler side stays in 2001, a new smokebox together with an LNER pattern chimney were fitted.

No. 63601 has visited other heritage lines including Keighley and Worth Valley and the Churnet Valley railways as well as Barrow Hill. It appeared at the National Railway Museum's Railfest 2012 event in June that year.

Its final run on the GCR came on June 24, 2012, its last passenger train arriving at Loughborough Central at 5.30pm.

By that time it had been based on the heritage era GCR for 16 years, five more than it had run in traffic for the original company.

After its withdrawal, talks with the National Railway Museum about a second overhaul for another decade on the GCR, or its future use as a static exhibit, began. The latter seems to be the most likely course of action for the forseeable future.

The three other O4s that survive are all in Australia.

Thirteen RODs were bought from the War Department during the 1920s by the mining firm of J&A Brown in New South Wales. J&A Brown operated the Richmond Vale Railway from a connection with the New South Wales Government Railways at Hexham to the Pelaw Main and Richmond Main collieries. No. 1984 is believed to have been last steamed in 1967 when the network was cut back.

Two of them, Nos. 20 and 24 (ROD Nos. 1984 and 2003), are owned by the Dorrigo

GCR O4 No. 63601 passes BR standard 2MT 2-6-0 No. 78019 as it enters Rothley with the Windcutter rake on October 9, 2006, during the annual autumn steam gala.
ROBIN JONES

Lining up alongside GER J17 0-6-0 No. 65567 at Barrow Hill Engine Shed's LNER II gala on April 3, 2009, are GCR O4 No. 63601 and Improved Director No. 506 *Butler-Henderson*. ROBIN JONES

O4 No. 63601 featured on one of six stamps issued by Royal Mail on January 12, 2004, to mark the bicentenary of the steam locomotive. Pop music producer Pete Waterman is pictured with a giant-sized version of the 28p stamp in front of the visiting O4 at the official launch of the set at the National Railway Museum. NRM

Steam Railway and Museum Limited in New South Wales.

The third survivor, No. 23, was initially located at Freeman's Waterhole in New South Wales as part of a mining display, but is now at the Richmond Vale Railway Museum.

To date, none of them has been restored to working order and while their service down under makes them part and parcel of Australian transport heritage, there have been enquiries about repatriating one or more to the UK, maybe for restoration in the livery of one of the companies other than the GCR or LNER.

A THIRD GCR LOCOMOTIVE?

At Loughborough's Golden Oldies spring gala at the end of May 2001, which featured replica locomotives from the dawn of the steam era, a project was launched to recreate a long-extinct class of original GCR locomotive at an estimated cost of £500,000.

The chosen locomotive was No. 567, originally a Manchester, Sheffield & Lincolnshire Railway Class 2 4-4-0 which once hauled express trains across the Woodhead route.

A cylinder block was found along with a GCR tender, the frames of which are suitable for reuse, at the Midland Railway-Butterley and taken to sister line the Great Central Railway (Nottingham)'s workshops at Ruddington Fields, while original Kitson drawings for the class were sourced at the

National Railway Museum.

The original No. 567 was one of a class of 31 locomotives built between 1887-94 at Kitson Works in Leeds and Gorton Works in Manchester.

Popular and economical locomotives, they survived into the LNER era where they became Class D7. The last was taken out of service and scrapped in 1939.

The project, being undertaken under the banner of the 567 Group, could be completed inside a decade, it was claimed.

A decision has been made to opt for an all-new boiler rather than modify an existing one.

The new locomotive will be based on the modern-day Great Central, but will be available to visit other heritage lines.

Group chairman Andrew Horrocks-Taylor said: "These elegant 4-4-0s were the pride of the MS&LR and then contributed towards the nascent GCR's slogan 'rapid travel in luxury'. Indeed the GCR's legendary first chairman Sir Edward Watkin was so pleased with his Class 2, that it was immortalised as the locomotive which features in the company crest.

"While we'll incorporate some minor changes, the new No. 567 will be externally indistinguishable from its predecessors."

The funding plan envisages 567 supporters signing up to give £5.67 a month for 10 years. Within days of the project launch at the GCR's spring steam gala, 50 supporters had signed up.

REBUILDING A COMPLETE GREAT CENTRAL TRAIN

According to the Vintage Carriage Trust's carriage survey, 11 original Great Central Railway passenger vehicles made it into preservation, including Grimsby & Immingham tramcar No. 14. There are also another eight from the company's Manchester, Sheffield & Lincolnshire Railway days.

The trust owns three 60ft 'Barnum' saloons and has a fourth on loan from the National Railway Museum.

Barnums entered service during 1910, marked the start of the final period of GCR passenger carriage design and broke all previous rules of construction and manufacture.

In 1905, four GCR officials visited the Washington Railroad Congress in the US. Robinson was impressed with his colleagues' report regarding US railroad practice and production engineering.

The Barnum nickname came from the design of the staff carriages built in Stoke for the American Barnum & Bailey circus touring train. Features in that design were repeated in the GCR carriages, giving them an American appearance.

The Barnums were built for excursion traffic at the GCR's new works at Dukinfield using the latest production methods.

Spacious, roomy and smooth riding, the Barnums made maximum use of the GCR's generous loading gauge, but as a result their use on certain other lines was restricted. They were allocated to London, Leicester,

Nottingham, Sheffield, Manchester and Mexborough.

Their arrival marked the introduction of a new livery. The first GCR two-tone colour scheme of dark oak and French white, subsequently replaced by dark oak and cream, had never proved practical. The teak that now took the place of the mahogany of the earlier panelled coaches has an oily surface which does not readily accept paint. Accordingly, Robinson decided that the new vehicles should have a natural finish protected by varnish.

Barnums lasted into BR days, the last being withdrawn in late 1958.

Withdrawn from passenger traffic, Nos. E5664 and E5666 were converted for use in departmental work. No. E5664 became Darlington tool van DE320540, while E5666, renumbered DE320709, was turned into a mobile workshop for the Peterborough area.

No. DE320540 first went to the Severn Valley Railway after being bought from British Rail in 1971. Sold again in 1979, it went to Loughborough before being acquired by the Main Line Steam Trust and moved to Ruddington.

No. DE320709 ended up being used as an office at Wrawby Junction on an isolated piece of track opposite the signalbox. It too found its way to Loughborough.

Barnum brake saloon originally numbered 695 became the Newcastle mess van, and in October 1970 moved to the embryonic North Yorkshire Moors Railway. After a restoration group there overhauled much of the running

Above: The overhaul of O4 No. 63601 entering its latter stages in Loughborough shed. ROBIN JONES

Below: Manchester, Sheffield & Lincolnshire Railway Class 2 (LNER D7) No. 567, to be replicated on the heritage-era Great Central. It is pictured when it was outshopped from Gorton Works in January 1891. 567 GROUP

The pair of ROD O4s stored at the Dorrigo Railway Museum in New South Wales. Might one or both ever return to the UK?
MIKE RUSSELL*

A Barnum coach stored under protective sheeting at Ruddington on the Great Central Railway (Nottingham). ANDREW HORROCKS-TAYLOR

A Barnum coach at the Nottingham Transport Heritage Centre at Ruddington. ROBIN JONES

Clerestory Composite Brake Lavatory No. 1663 at Ruddington is the oldest surviving Great Central Railway vehicle (from after the Manchester, Sheffield & Lincolnshire Railway era). ROBIN JONES

Much to be done, but by no means impossible: the interior of a Barnum coach at Ruddington. ANDREW HORROCKS-TAYLOR

gear, it too ended up at Ruddington Fields.

The fourth preserved Barnum, No. 228, was retrieved from Alexandra Docks in Hull where the Hull Docks Engineers had turned it into a tomato hothouse. It arrived at Ruddington in October 1997 and substantial work has been progressed on it since.

Also at Ruddington is the body of clerestory Composite Brake Lavatory No. 1663 of 1903, which had been used as a canteen at Hull Kingston Rovers Craven Park ground. It's the oldest surviving Great Central carriage and is currently mounted on the underframe of a LMS BG which has now become its permanent rolling chassis.

As highlighted opposite, trust volunteers have been progressing with Manchester Sheffield & Lincolnshire Railway six-wheel five-compartment carriage No. 946, which finished up at Stratford locomotive works where it was used as a boiler tube store before being damaged in a Territorial Army exercise.

Suburban non-corridor eight-compartment Third No. 799 was built in 1905 to a Robinson design and survived in departmental use before use by the Hull Docks Engineer.

A Craven Suburban Third brake body of 1905/06 was retrieved from Armthorpe, near Doncaster, after being used for more than half a century in an orchard garden. It has many original fittings such as door hinges, leather straps for the droplights, side ventilators and heavily wallpapered internal partitions including graffiti from the 1920s, detailing the latest Yorkshire cricket scores! It needs major restoration as well as a new underframe.

The body of Robinson eight-compartment Suburban Third No. 793, also dating from 1905, has been cosmetically restored to protect it from further deterioration, and is stored at Swithland Sidings. It is the only original GCR coach on the Loughborough to Leicester North section.

Progress of the restoration of these historically priceless vehicles has been slow and is being carried out in stages as funds permit.

The preservation sector has seen many miracles worked in the restoration of pre-Grouping wooden-bodied coaches, the long-time market leaders in the field being the Bluebell and Isle of Wight Steam railways.

The concept of a complete GCR train in the

REMEMBERING
BRITAIN'S WORST RAIL DISASTER

Far left: Manchester, Sheffield & Lincolnshire Railway six-wheeler No. 946 being rebuilt at Ruddington. CLYDE PENNINGTON

Left: The high quality marquetry on the restored seating. CLYDE PENNINGTON

Volunteers are restoring a Victorian coach to provide a memorial to Britain's worst ever rail disaster.

Manchester, Sheffield & Lincolnshire Railway six-wheeler No. 946, which was built in 1888, is approaching the latter stages of its restoration by the GCR Rolling Stock Trust at the Nottingham Transport Heritage Centre.

It is one of the last of this type of carriage left in Britain, and it is hoped that its restoration will help piece together some of the key reasons for the worst ever rail accident in Britain.

Restorers aim to have the vehicle ready for display in May 2015, the centenary of the disaster. No. 946 was rescued from scrapping, having served its latter days as a boiler shop store and a hunters' lodge on a Cambridgeshire farm before being acquired by the trust in 2000. The restoration of the wooden

body and the running gear has been painstakingly progressed since then.

In May 1915, more than 400 men of the Royal Scots Regiment, on their way to the Gallipoli Campaign from Scotland, were killed or severely burned in a most horrific disaster at Quintinshill near Gretna Green.

Due to a signalman's error, their troop train was in collision with four other trains on the West Coast Main Line. Much of the troop train was assembled from a rake of six-wheel wooden-bodied carriages built at Gorton by the then MSLR.

John Quick, the trust's GCR historian, said: "Our need was to help understand why the fire killed so many soldiers of the Royal Scots Regiment; how it could have started and why far more did not escape the resulting inferno?"

Pat Sumner, a former BR carriage engineer, said: "This type of wooden-

bodied carriage was carrying a large gas cylinder to provide lighting.

"All the carriage doors were reported locked to prevent passengers jumping or falling out, and the upholstery would have generated a thick blanket of smothering and toxic smoke as each carriage caught fire. The fire of course made the gas pipes and tanks explode, causing a massive inferno – which then spread to the other trains involved."

John Quick added: "The Great Central was the last of the big Victorian railways and in some ways one of the most innovative due to tough competition from other railway companies and the burgeoning use of the internal combustion engine in cars and commercial vehicles.

"We have a massive job to do to restore these classic carriages. Once lost they are gone for ever."

21st century may well need substantial grant aid to make it happen sooner rather than later; but when it happens, it will not only be a star attraction in its own right but also a major educational resource.

The Buckinghamshire Railway Centre is home to 1916-built GCR Robinson Suburban Brake Third No. 652, which ended its days in departmental use as No. TDE320603. It moved to Quainton Road in 1997, and is also undergoing restoration.

Still very much in use, but as static holiday accommodation, is Ashbury First Class carriage No. 957, which was once based at the Buckinghamshire Railway Centre after surviving in departmental service as No. E5957E. It is now one of two coaches available for hire at Brockford Sidings, which has been set up on the trackbed of the Mid-Suffolk Light Railway.

MANCHESTER, SHEFFIELD & LINCS RAILWAY SURVIVORS

Several Manchester, Sheffield & Lincolnshire Railway six-wheelers have survived, some complete with full frame and running gear, others as bodies only.

The latest donation to the Ruddington-based rolling stock trust is six-wheel five-compartment No. 373, built at Gorton in 1889. Converted by the LNER in the Thirties for use as camping coach No. 35 at Royal Deeside, it was rescued in the 1970s and moved to Ruddington from the East Anglia Ra

A complete six-wheeler is housed at the Buckinghamshire Railway Centre, having been restored for some years, but the original running number is uncertain, while a Brake Third body mounted on a modern chassis is in regular service at the Chasewater Railway.

Tricomposite luggage compartment No. 154,

which dates from 1876, was restored from its latter-day use as a stores van by the Vintage Carriages Trust based at Ingrow. It jointly won an Association of Railway Preservation Society coach award.

Tanfield Railway No. 8 comprises the body of 1885-built four-wheel four-compartment Brake Third mounted on a much later chassis. It is in regular service.

Also at Tanfield is the body of six-wheel Family Saloon No. 1506, which was built in 1899, and which is awaiting restoration.

The body of a four-wheel First (later Composite) built 1880 for the Manchester South Junction & Altrincham Railway, which ended up on the Isle of Wight in 1913 as Freshwater, Yarmouth & Newport Railway No. 6, spent 76 years as a chalet at Wooton from 1930. It is now at the Isle of Wight Steam Railway awaiting restoration. ■

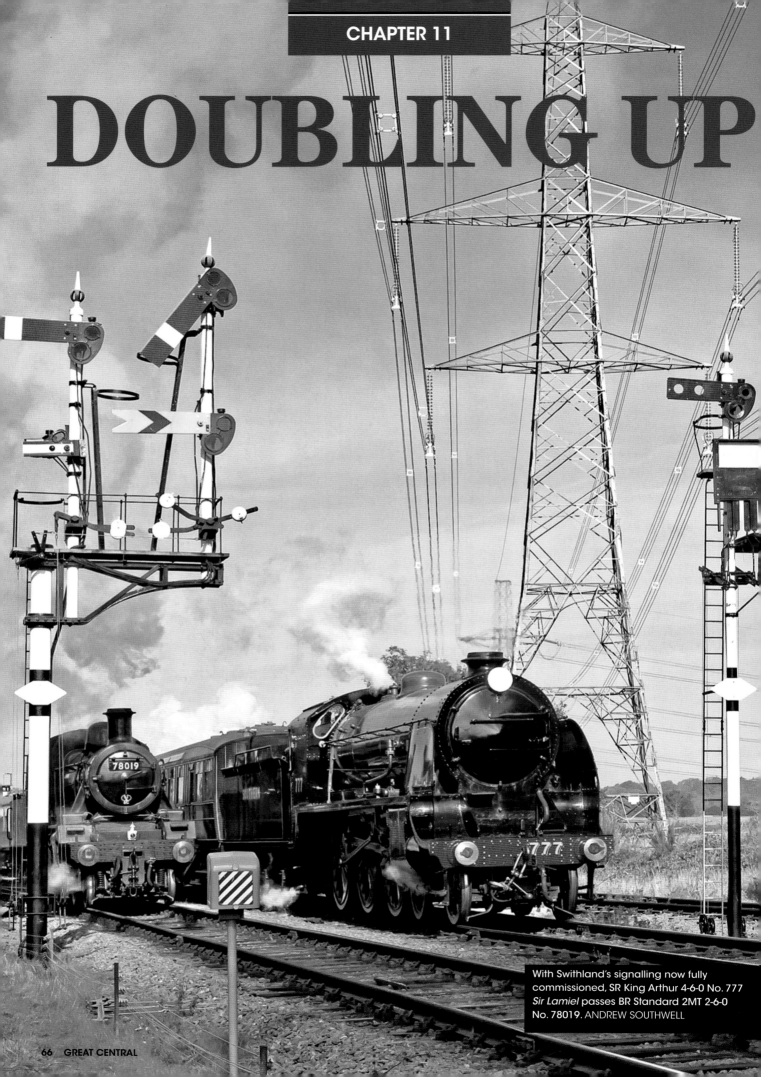

CHAPTER 11

DOUBLING UP

With Swithland's signalling now fully commissioned, SR King Arthur 4-6-0 No. 777 *Sir Lamiel* passes BR Standard 2MT 2-6-0 No. 78019. ANDREW SOUTHWELL

LNER A4 Pacific No. 60007 *Sir Nigel Gresley* leaves Quorn & Woodhouse on October 15, 1994, during the autumn gala. It had been repainted into BR blue at Rothley. The double track by now had progressed sufficiently to provide a main line image over a substantial part of the railway. JOHN EAST

June 1, 2000, marked one of the biggest milestones in 50 years of British preservation – the formal opening of the Great Central Railway's double track main line between Loughborough and Rothley.

And it was all down to the realisation of a boyhood dream.

David Clarke, aged 10, was invited to join his uncle Archibald and learn all about signalling in his 'box at Ruislip and Ickenham, afterwards railways became his number one passion in life.

He would visit the signalbox on the line shared by the GWR and Great Central at every available opportunity to learn the ropes.

After his uncle passed away from a heart attack at the age of 63 in 1943, young David had mastered the art and as his in-depth knowledge was held in such high regard by fellow signalmen he was allowed to regularly work a turn in their 'boxes.

Did that schoolboy back on that first visit in 1940 ever believe that one day he would pull a lever to send the first train off on his 'own' main line?

For that is exactly what happened 60 years later, at Rothley signalbox as David, a contemporary of Stirling Moss, made his fortune from motor racing and dealing with Ferrari cars.

David's parents, Arnold and Ivy Clarke, ran a successful box manufacturing company in Mountsorrel, which inspired their son with a passion for all things mechanical, especially Ferraris.

His collection grew and he employed mechanics to renovate his collection, and he was soon approached by other Ferrari owners

The realisation of a boyhood dream: the GCR's late benefactor David Clarke signals trains on to the Down main at Rothley on June 1, 2000. He financed the project with a "considerable" six-figure sum. ROBIN JONES

As the double track neared completion, the GCR could recreate even more realistic main line settings. Southern Railway King Arthur 4-6-0 No. 30777 *Sir Lamiel* and B1 4-6-0 No. 1264 depart Quorn & Woodhouse in 1998. JOHN EAST

WR 4-6-0 No. 6990 *Witherslack Hall* takes the Down main from Leicester North into Rothley for the official double-track opening ceremony on June 1, 2000. ROBIN JONES

The main line image is again portrayed in style as LNER A2 Pacific No. 60532 *Blue Peter* approaches Quorn during a photo charter on March 18, 1999.

asking him to work on their cars. The factory at Mountsorrel provided a workshop space for the business named Graypaul.

The business was awarded main dealer status and moved to Loughborough. Eventually, he sold the business to the Otford group, freeing up David's time and resources to fund the double-track project.

On the day of its completion, David proudly raised the signal to allow GWR 4-6-0 No. 6990 *Witherslack Hall* running back to Loughborough from Leicester North on to the new Down main.

It was the final realisation of an ambition, which David, who became GCR president, had held since he joined the heritage line in 1976. At that time he became captivated with the revivalists' aims, and made a "very substantial" shares application and an open-handed offer to help. Recalling school holidays spent trainspotting at Swithland (David's family lived at nearby Mountsorrel), the double-track project was his brainchild.

He set out to recreate the atmosphere of a typical signalbox on the Chiltern Line, complete with double track and long passing loops, and was one of the few people on the line to have a pedigree of having worked on the original CCR main line.

From drawing board to final implementation, the doubling scheme took 10 years. And it gave the GCR a unique position as the only double-track heritage main line in the country... and probably the world.

The project started with the clearance of the Swithland sidings site, which in 1990 was a wasteland, with only the former Up line running through and a ruined building. Track was initially laid on the previous down line formation from the north end of Rothley and through Swithland, loops being added on both down and up sides of the line there.

David hired contractor B Trackwork of Doncaster to lay the first half-mile of double track in 1992, from Rothley to Swithland, followed by an extension north to Kinchley Lane bridge.

After that, Nick Tinsley and Geoff Parton took over the project, laying the track materials financed by David.

Quorn & Woodhouse was reached by the second line in 1996, and limited public passenger services between Quorn and Swithland began the following year using a DMU.

In 1999, the Down main reached back to Loughborough Central, a total length of 5½ miles. Ballasting and tamping finished just 10 weeks before the official opening, with the first train running over the Down main a fortnight before the official opening.

EFFORTS PRAISED

At the official opening at 11.40am on June 1, chief executive, Graham Oliver, told the crowd of VIPs and invited guests on Rothley platform that the GCR was likely to remain the only double-track main line in preservation, and praised the efforts of all those who had helped make it happen.

National Railway Museum head of engineering collections, Richard Gibbons, who stood on the steps of Rothley 'box as David pulled the lever, said: "It was lovely to be participating in what was such an important historic event and for two of our locomotives, the O4 and No. 60800 *Green Arrow*, to be taking a prominent role on the day."

The climax of the opening ceremony came when David pulled a sequence of levers to operate signals 17, 18 and 19 to send the nine-coach train on its way. The first passing of trains on the line came about 20 minutes later, when the VIP train heading for Loughborough crossed paths with Robinson 04 No. 63601 hauling the 'Windcutter' rake of 16-ton mineral wagons south from Quorn & Woodhouse.

Multi-millionaire David, who ran his own charity, the Shuttlewood-Clarke Foundation, for handicapped, disabled and elderly people, said: "I regret not having become involved with the GCR sooner than I did.

"If I had come on to the scene earlier I would have had double-track line all the way into Leicester Central. That is now impossible because the bridges have all been taken out, so the double-track project was the next best thing."

The total cost of the doubling project was around £1.2 million, the Main Line Steam Trust, raising a significant slice of the finance.

The grand opening brought immediate benefits, for the following Saturday, June 3, saw at Loughborough Central a renewed hive of activity as enthusiasts and the public alike turned up in droves following the media publicity.

"The atmosphere at Quorn was just like a main line station in the Sixties when you went trainspotting and could see a train movement every 20 minutes," said Graham. "We started out 30 years ago to recreate a main line steam railway and a lot of people said it was an impossible dream. I am totally delighted that we have proved them wrong."

Graham paid tribute to former GCR chairmen John Kirby, Richard Willis, Bruce Lovatt and

GER J15 0-6-0 No. 65462 enters Quorn & Woodhouse with a demonstration freight from Loughborough on January 24, 2004, during the 'Mail by Rails' gala. The award-winning signalling scheme at the station was given HM Railway Inspectorate approval in time to be used at the event. BRIAN DEAN

The double track allowed trains to pass on an authentic main line. In April 2004, visiting GWR small prairie No. 5553 approaches Rothley, while large prairie No. 4141 waits to depart for Loughborough. IAN LOASBY

An hour before his sudden death, David Clarke prepares for lunch aboard the GCR's first-class restaurant car on July 27, 2002. SUSAN SANSOME/GCR

deputy chairman Fred Herrick – all of whom had passed away – for their roles in the line's success. But, he said, without Bill Ford, who formed the shareholding company Great Central Railway and raised £70,000 to save the line in 1976, there would not be a Great Central today.

When contemplating the GCR's achievements made by the turn of the century, by numerous voluntary contributions big and small in terms of time, effort and money, who would have been the most proud, that little boy or his uncle at Ruislip?

The project had been taking shape over the previous decade, each step further reinforcing the GCR's position as a main line rather than a 'starter' preserved railway that relied on industrial locomotives.

GROWING IN STATURE

At the same time, the status of the GCR as a main line in preservation was growing by the year. In January 1993, rebuilt Bulleid West Country light Pacific No. 34039 *Boscastle* returned to traffic from ex-Barry condition after 21 years – at the time, the longest restoration programme on the railway.

That year, LMS 'Black Five' No. 45231 had been specially 'dirtied down' for the film *Shadowlands* starring Anthony Hopkins and Debra Winger. It was the first major location filming contract since the Great Train Robbery epic *Buster* starring Phil Collins in the previous decade; the line by then had become a premium choice for film makers, largely because of its authentic setting.

In 1994, the GCR was graced by the visits of LNER A4 Pacific No. 60007 *Sir Nigel Gresley*, which had been repainted into BR blue at Rothley shed, and the NRM's rebuilt Princess Coronation Pacific No. 46229 *Duchess of Hamilton*.

Meanwhile, several staged extensions of the track saw Quorn & Woodhouse reached in 1996. The completed Down line between Quorn and Rothley was used for works trains, photographic specials and for acceptance testing of 1500v DC locomotives built for the Hong Kong Metro.

On the second track, limited public passenger working back in 1997 used a DMU between Quorn and Swithland.

The laying of the second track was carried out to meticulous detail. Before laying the track, the formation was excavated and new bottom ballast laid.

The railway laid flat-bottom rail on concrete sleepers is to minimise maintenance and maximise strength, the railway having a 25-ton axle loading for running the heaviest locomotives.

ONWARDS TO LOUGHBOROUGH

Work began on doubling the line between Quorn and Loughborough in January 1997, with the excavation of the former Down line formation. The dirty ballast excavated was taken to Swithland sidings where it was cleaned. After that it was returned to form the bottom ballast for the new track. The work took just two weeks for the two mile-stretch, and between Quorn and Swithland, the double track was laid by a pair of works trains, one hauled by the Gresley N2 0-6-2T No. 69523.

The redundant signalbox retrieved at the south end of Aylesbury station was rebuilt at Swithland with a new brick base. Next to the signalbox, a relay room and mess building was constructed, designed in a style not unlike the original buildings on the line.

The former goods shed was restored for use as signal and telegraph department workshop, and extensive sidings were laid for stock storage. Swithland sidings is seen as a jewel in the crown of the double-track project. The sidings represent a quadruple track section of

the former Great Western/Great Central Joint Line from Northolt Junction in the south to Ashenden Junction in the north, as David Clarke had remembered it.

The sidings had been laid initially laid by the original GCR and opened in 1898. Its main purpose was to deal with the granite trains from the Mountsorrel quarries via the industrial branch line to the east. Goods trains would collect the granite wagons from the quarry, remarshal them in the sidings according to their destination and progress on to the main line. Returning empties would be similarly dealt with.

The Up and Down main lines near the sidings were spaced to allow for the building of another island platform similar to that at Rothley and Quorn & Woodhouse, but this was never built. However, it is still possible to see the bricked-up station entrance on the bridge over The Ridings.

During the Second World War, considerable enhancements were made to the railway in preparation for the D-Day landings. Work was carried out in the yard at Quorn & Woodhouse station and at Swithland and extra track was built across The Ridings.

With the final closure of the route in 1969, British Rail lifted all the sidings as well as the second main line.

It was therefore left to the revivalists to create what is the largest track and signalling project anywhere in railway preservation.

However, the most complex element of the project was the remodelling of the south end of Loughborough station. Points and two carriage sidings capable of holding 14 coaches were laid. Two brick relay rooms were built in Great Central style for the signalling, necessary for the power working of the complicated layout, including nine motor-worked points. Installation of the mechanical signalling at Loughborough is approaching completion.

TRAGEDY AT THE SUMMER GALA

It was estimated that David provided around £1.5 million towards this project, which sadly, he never saw fully completed; with all of the signalling in place and operational. He collapsed and died from a massive heart attack

LMS 'Jinty' 0-6-0T No. 47406 passes the array of signalling soon to be commissioned at Swithland sidings on the Great Central Railway on February 12, 2012. ALAN WEAVER

on a train during the line's July 27-28, 2002, steam gala, at the age of 72.

David had been at the gala on Saturday, July 27, from early morning, taking breakfast with then general manager Graham Oliver as he had done on more than 500 weekly occasions since 1989, when he became president.

He travelled in coach restoration group Railway Vehicle Preservation's newly outshopped 1959-built Royal Mail Travelling Post Office which had just won a local award for the standard of renovation, and then rode on the line's lunchtime dining trains with a group of friends.

Loughborough stationmaster Brian Axon escorted him to the 3pm departure to Leicester North, and David intended to disembark at Rothley where he had left his car.

However, shortly after the train pulled out of Rothley, a member of the RVP selling postcards had found David slumped below a window.

The ticket inspector and guard arrived on the scene and an ambulance was called and two nurses responded to a request for assistance, but they could detect no pulse.

A waiting ambulance at Leicester North took David to Leicester Royal Infirmary where he was pronounced dead on arrival.

The medical emergency caused delays to the timetable at Leicester North, but it was not until well in the evening that stunned GCR staff, volunteers and friends of David became aware of what had happened.

Graham, his friend of 27 years, said: "He was the man who took on board the GCR dream – and made it happen. The last thing he saw before he died was Swithland sidings and

The GCR's resident Class 101 DMU was used to test the signalling at Swithland before commissioning on May 30, 2012. It is seen entering the Down loop using a 'calling on arm' on the Down home bracket. STEVE TAYLOR

signalbox, which would not have been there without his help.

"On the last day he was alive, a man came up to us and said he had just visited 19 preserved railways around the country and felt that the GCR was the best. David was very proud when he heard that."

Following his death, the GCR launched an emergency appeal to pay off its overdraft, which David had personally guaranteed. The railway's supporting charity, The David Clarke Railway Trust, was founded in his memory.

A STUNNING SUCCESS

The double track immediately provided additional capacity which became especially useful at galas, where up to six trains may be in operation at any one time. It also facilitated the running of non-passenger carrying trains such as demonstration freights and the line's TPO set during galas to a greater extent than any other heritage railway.

Furthermore, HM Railway Inspectorate has granted powers to run private test trains at up to 60mph, as opposed to the maximum speed

Newly acquired BR Standard 9F No. 92214, 'dirtied up' for a special Swithland sidings gala on May 11, 2014, as it departs Loughborough with a demonstration freight. ROBIN JONES

BR Standard 9F 2-10-0 No. 92214
pauses at Swithland sidings
signalbox on May 11, 2014, during a
special gala.
ROBIN JONES

Visiting GWR heavy freight 2-8-0 No. 3802 passes Kinchley Lane with the railway's 'windcutter' rake of 16 ton mineral wagons during the winter steam gala on a snowbound January 26, 2013.

of 25mph on other lines. On March 20, 2004, a new signalbox at Quorn & Woodhouse was officially opened by Pete Waterman. He unveiled a Westinghouse signalling award plaque, which the railway had won in the previous year's National Rail Heritage Awards, and pulled the signal to allow an express train to pass through the station at speed.

It is the only preserved signalbox in Britain with a double track on either side, and enabled a train to be despatched from Loughborough every 10 minutes.

The 'box came from Market Rasen in Lincolnshire and was re-erected and made operational again at a cost of hundreds of thousands of pounds.

Four miles of metal wire connects the levers in the 'box to the signals and there is around one-and-a-half miles of electrical wiring inside the 'box alone!

A further signalbox at Swithland sidings was fitted with signals in the style of the GCR/GWR joint line via High Wycombe, making a further increase in capacity possible.

The full Swithland signalling project was completed in May 2012. In December that year, the GCR was again awarded the NRHA Signalling Award for the project. Swithland now forms the centrepiece of the double track. GCR managing director, Bill Ford, said: "We are immensely proud to collect this award. It is a tribute to our team who completed the project to such a high standard,

the fundraisers who helped make it a reality and most of all to the late David Clarke, the man who inspired and provided a large amount of funding for the project. He had a passion for signalling and while he never lived

to see Swithland signalbox commissioned, I am sure he would have been extremely impressed.

"His vision is now an educational legacy for future generations."

Kinchley Lane, south of Quorn & Woodhouse station, is one of the most popular locations for photography in the entire UK heritage railway portfolio, and is an 'easy' place to capture the double-track main line at its finest. Telegraph poles have been positioned to recreate the steam-era ambience of the spot, reached by a muddy lane which becomes packed at gala events. BR Standard 2MT 2-6-0 No. 78019 is seen heading south to Rothley. ROBIN JONES

CHAPTER 12

A new flagship

BR Standard Britannia Pacific No. 70013 *Oliver Cromwell* heads past Kinchley Lane on May 3, 2008, with its first passenger train since the 'Fifteen Guinea Special' of August 11, 1968. DEREK BILLINGS

Craig Stinchcombe, the GCR's chief engineer (front), and locomotive engineering manager Tom Tighe on the footplate of *Oliver Cromwell* at the rededication ceremony. ROBIN JONES

On May 10, 2008, a very special occasion was marked by the Great Central Railway. For it was at Loughborough on that day that the parliamentary under secretary of state for transport, Tom Harris, officially launched preservation icon BR Britannia Pacific No. 70013 *Oliver Cromwell* into traffic, in the company of staff of owner National Railway Museum.

The locomotive, which had undergone a restoration lasting four years at Loughborough shed, is a defining symbol of the heritage railway movement, as it was one of the engines to haul the fabled 'Fifteen Guinea Special' of August 11, 1968; the last steam-hauled standard gauge passenger train run by British Rail. No. 70013 had not hauled a main line passenger train in the 40 years since.

In the run-up to the date in May, the unveiling of its nameplates had followed a race to have No. 70013 back in service in time for the GCR's May 3-5, steam gala.

Following the lifting of the boiler back into its frames on April 10, after passing steam and hydraulic tests, paid staff and volunteers had worked round the clock to reassemble the locomotive in Loughborough shed.

On Sunday, April 27, its cladding back on and the locomotive repainted in Brunswick green with new number transfers being applied, it was hauled out of the works by a diesel shunter to have its valves set.

Following its rededication, *Oliver Cromwell*

took pride of place at the National Railway Museum's nine-day 1968 And All That 40th anniversary commemoration of the end of main line steam at York on May 24-June 1.

Over the decades, *Oliver Cromwell* had become the Holy Grail of the heritage movement. GCR general manager Robert Crew said that when news of its resteaming broke, enthusiasts travelled to Loughborough from as far afield as Canada and Costa Rica to see it.

Oliver Cromwell, which had been outshopped from Crewe works on May 30, 1951, and initially allocated to Norwich shed, was virtually assured of preservation when it became the last standard gauge steam engine to be overhauled for British Rail, at Crewe between October 1966 and February 1967.

It continued in regular use with the other last few survivors of the class which had numbered 55, operating from Carlisle Kingmoor shed until it closed to steam at the end of 1967.

All of the last surviving Britannias were withdrawn from Kingmoor, with the exception of No. 70013, which was moved to Carnforth, where it was stored under a tarpaulin, and only emerged for very occasional railtour duties during the first few months of 1968.

It was British Rail's last working Pacific, and its last standard gauge named steam locomotive. In fact, apart from *Flying Scotsman*, it was the only Pacific to haul passenger trains of any description in 1968 as

The National Railway Museum's former head of knowledge and collections, Helen Ashby, and MP Tom Harris launch *Oliver Cromwell* back into service on May 10, 2008. ROBIN JONES

BR had introduced a ban on the operation of privately owned steam engines on its tracks at the end of 1967.

Demand for *Oliver Cromwell* for use on the railtours in the north-west marking the end of steam traction on the main line, naturally increased as the final curtain approached, and it was always inevitable that No. 70013 would be selected to haul the last train, handling the Manchester Victoria to Carlisle leg of the 'Fifteen Guinea Special' of August 11. *Oliver Cromwell* was turned at Carlisle and ran light engine, following the LMS 'Black Five' – hauled special south over the Settle & Carlisle line, continuing overnight via Doncaster and March; its one-time home shed, to arrive at Norwich on the Monday afternoon.

After withdrawal, *Oliver Cromwell* – as part of the National Collection – found a new home at Bressingham Steam Museum following a meeting between founder the late Alan Bloom and David Ward, then Eastern Region divisional commercial manager.

No. 70013 steamed again the following month – giving rides on the museum's 200-yard standard gauge demonstration line, where it ran until 1973. It had been silent ever since.

In 1993, would-be restorers reached agreement with the NRM for No. 70013 to be released, and launched a nationwide appeal to pay for its overhaul, but there was opposition to it leaving the Norfolk venue on the grounds that it was a major draw for visitors, and the

Just after arriving from Bressingham, *Oliver Cromwell* proudly stands at Loughborough station. BRIAN SHARPE

Complete with 32A Norwich shedplate, No. 70013 *Oliver Cromwell* departs from Chesterfield on June 9, 1968 with a railtour that marked the closure of the Midland Railway route across the Pennines between Derby and Manchester. JEFF COLLEDGE

On August 10, 2008, just as it did 40 years almost to the day before, No. 70013 *Oliver Cromwell* departed Manchester Victoria at 11.06, with its first passenger working since the original 1T57 'Fifteen Guinea Special'. It is seen passing the remains of Manchester Exchange. BRIAN SHARPE

Out in the Loughborough sunshine for the first time since its repaint, *Oliver Cromwell*, minus its smoke deflectors, has its valves reset in late April 2008.

Loughborough shed staff worked round the clock in April 2008 to have *Oliver Cromwell* ready for the early May gala. ROBIN JONES

museum would suffer financially if it left. Bloom asked the NRM to provide an exhibit of similar significance in exchange, such as LNER V2 2-6-2 No. 4771 *Green Arrow* or another engine of similar stature.

However, the then head of the NRM, Andrew Dow, said that it was not for a borrower to decide the terms under which a National Collection item could be returned.

Nonetheless, Bloom stuck to his guns, stating that *Oliver Cromwell* had arrived at the Diss museum on "permanent loan" – a clause which had never been successfully challenged by the NRM – and which also predated the establishment of the York museum. The stalemate was not broken, and all money raised towards that appeal was returned to the donors.

A decade passed, and in early 2004, agreement was reached for *Oliver Cromwell* to be overhauled to MT276 main line standard – and returned to steam, hopefully, by 2008. The NRM sent *Green Arrow* to Bressingham in exchange.

No. 70013 was taken from its home of 36 years at Bressingham to be taken to the NRM as a major exhibit in the Railfest 2004 steam bicentenary festival, which ran from May 29 to June 6.

Afterwards, it was taken to Loughborough shed in readiness for an overhaul costing in the region of £100,000, again supported by a nationwide appeal for donations. A substantial five-figure sum was raised within days of its launch.

The overhaul was carried out by members of the Loughborough Standard Locomotive Group and 5305 Locomotive Association, which jointly committed to carry out the overhaul work for free under the direction of GCR locomotive engineer Tom Tighe.

During an *Oliver Cromwell* gala weekend arranged at short notice following its rededication, No. 70013 heads out of Loughborough past Woodthorpe Lane on May 18, 2008. GARETH GRIFFITHS

In announcing the restoration agreement, David Ward, who had become chairman of the board of trustees at Bressingham, said: "We are delighted to be a full partner in the project to return *Oliver Cromwell* to steam and see it working all over Britain."

Following its overhaul, Helen Ashby, head of knowledge and collections at the NRM, thanked Bressingham Steam Museum for looking after No. 70013 since its withdrawal in 1968, and for agreeing to release the locomotive for restoration.

No. 70013 made a swift return to the main line, undergoing test runs in July 2008 before heading a series of charters, the first of which was on August 11 that year. Its first mainline passenger charter since 1968 on August 10, 2008 was no less than a rerun of the 'Fifteen Guinea Special'. It then hauled the 'Scarborough Spa Express' later in the month.

On September 9, 2008, *Oliver Cromwell* completed a rerun of 'The Norfolkman', running from Liverpool Street to Norwich and back again, visiting the site of its former home of Norwich shed, and carrying an appropriate 32A shedplate on the smokebox.

On November 8 that year, the locomotive was temporarily renumbered as sister engine 70048 and renamed *The Territorial Army 1908-2008* to mark the 100th anniversary of the Territorial Army. The naming was performed by seasoned GCR visitor HRH The Duke of Gloucester at Quorn & Woodhouse station. During the 2008 renaming, No. 70013 carried this name on the right-hand side smoke deflector as a link with its past association with the Territorial Army.

More history was made on May 23, 2009, when the locomotive hauled a railtour from Norwich to Poole in Dorset before travelling to the Swanage Railway under its own power,

Michael Gregory from Cromwell Tools, whose company supported the restoration, along with the 'Cromwell Pullman' headboard carried by the engine on its VIP launch at Loughborough on May 10, 2008. ROBIN JONES

via Wareham and the reinstated link between the national network and the heritage line at Motala.

On March 11, 2010, *Oliver Cromwell* hauled the opening railtour over the newly reinstated level crossing at Sheringham on the North Norfolk Railway, arriving from King's Cross, via Cambridge and Norwich. The missing level crossing was long considered to be in the same category as the lost bridge over the Midland Main Line at Loughborough – one of the biggest blockages in the heritage sector.

No. 70013 remains one of the most popular main line performers to this day, and regularly returns to its Loughborough base to haul GCR services. ∎

CHAPTER 13

The testing of *Tornado*

One of the biggest honours bestowed on the modern-day Great Central Railway came when it was chosen as the testbed for *Tornado*, the first new main line steam locomotive built for service in Britain in nearly half a century.

The previous one had been British Railways Standard 9F 2-10-0 No. 92220 *Evening Star*, which emerged in a blaze of publicity from Swindon Works in 1960.

It was in 1990 that a group of enthusiasts launched a project to recreate an extinct, but hugely popular, class of LNER Pacific, in the form of the 50th Arthur Peppercorn A1.

Named in honour of the RAF Tornado crews flying at the time in the Gulf War, it was numbered 60163, next in the class after No. 60162 *Saint Johnstoun*. It took 18 years for the group, which became The A1 Steam Locomotive Trust, to take the project from conception to its first steaming.

Costing a total of £3 million to build, *Tornado* moved under its own power for the first time on July 29, 2008 at the trust's base at Hopetown Carriage Works, next to Darlington North Road station.

On August 7, 2008, *Tornado* was entered onto the Total Operations Processing System

(TOPS). Although the painted number is 60163, on the British network it is designated No. 98863 in TOPS. Ninety-eight describes a steam engine, the 'eight' stems from the power classification of 8P(1), and '63' comes from its 'official' number 60163.

Still in grey undercoat, *Tornado* was taken by two articulated lorries to the GCR for two months of testing at speeds of up to 60mph. It was decided that the new A1 would remain in 'works grey' until final testing was completed, as a precaution against the need to remove the boiler cladding.

While in this undercoat, it wore the web

Next stop Leicester North! *Tornado* heads a second covenantors' special on September 21, 2008. ROBIN JONES

History being made on the Great Central: *Tornado* enters Quorn & Woodhouse after bringing its empty coaching stock from Loughborough on September 21, 2008. ROBIN JONES

address of the A1 Trust on the side of the tender, and the mark RA9, denoting route availability on the locomotive cab.

Tornado arrived on the GCR on August 19, 2008, and was unloaded in Quorn & Woodhouse yard the following day, before being towed to Loughborough shed.

Its fire was lit that evening, and following a 'fitness-to-run' examination on the morning of August 21 it made two light engine runs that afternoon, including its first non-stop mile run.

The next day, *Tornado's* vacuum brakes were tested and then it hauled the GCR's directors' saloon down the line, propelling it back to Loughborough, from where it coupled up to its first train and completed two empty coaching stock round trips to Leicester North.

There then followed the GCR's Thomas the Tank Engine-themed bank holiday weekend of August 23-25. *Tornado* joined in the fun by wearing a plastic face and made light runs during the event.

Following HM Railway Inspectorate approval for the tests, *Tornado* effortlessly achieved 60mph running with empty passenger stock comprising test trains of 500 tons, and without fault.

September 10 saw the loco have its first official timing as it hauled 518 tons up the 1-in-176 gradient running south from Rothley station.

Finally, the big day came when *Tornado* made its debut on fully fledged passenger trains. Permission was given after HMRI had

given its approval the previous week, following a loaded test run when *Tornado* hauled 11 coaches and a 'dead' Class 45 Peak diesel.

On September 21, it backed on to an eight-coach train formed of three red and cream-liveried coaches, four green-liveried coaches, and, at the rear, the line's restored LNER Beavertail observation car.

Tornado departed at 10.15am from Quorn & Woodhouse, running nonstop to Leicester North, back to Loughborough, and then returned to Quorn.

Among the VIPs on board were original trust chairman David Champion, whose dog Bud wore a coat with 60163 sewn into it.

In the superb sunshine and summer-like temperatures on the first day of autumn,

Raw power of an A1: *Tornado* waits to haul its first load of passengers from Quorn & Woodhouse on September 21. ROBIN JONES

Running light engine, No. 60163 passes between semaphore signals beyond Loughborough station on March 21, 2010, while making its return visit to the Great Central. ALAN WEAVER/A1 TRUST

Tornado runs round its train at Leicester North on September 21, 2008. ROBIN JONES

crowds gathered on the station platforms and overbridges to glimpse both transport history being made, and a locomotive all set to become to 21st-century steam what *Flying Scotsman* was to the 20th.

The trips went faultlessly, and nobody on board had anything but admiration for *Tornado* and the team that built it at Darlington.

Another four trains hauled by *Tornado* ran that day, and up to 2000 trust supporters and guests were carried.

The fare-paying public had their chance

the next day (September 22), with more than 1000 passengers being carried on the three sold-out trips.

On October 4, it carried a special headboard during a special commemorative event marking the 125th anniversary of the Boys' Brigade, hauling the GCR's Travelling Post Office rake.

Still in grey primer, *Tornado* stole the limelight in that year's October 10-12 autumn steam gala, which had a 'big engines' theme, and was the most successful event of its kind

in the line's history to date. Lured by the spectacle of the brand new A1, around 7000 passengers travelled, with seven-coach trains running full to standing room only. At one point on the Saturday, police closed the road leading to Quorn & Woodhouse station because of the huge number of queuing cars .

Tornado was joined by BR Britannia Pacific No. 70013 *Oliver Cromwell*, SR 4-6-0 No. 850 *Lord Nelson*, and LMS Jubilee 4-6-0 No. 5690 *Leander*.

A special guest was His Honour Edgar Fay QC, the son of the original GCR general manager Sir Sam Fay, who celebrated his 100th birthday at the event from the comfort of the dining train.

The beer tent entered the spirit of the event with four specially brewed ales – *Tornado*, *Cromwell*, *Nelson* and *Leander*! However, the LMS design was the first one to sell out.

GCR president Bill Ford said: "This was a wonderful one-off. With Britain's brand new main line steam engine *Tornado*, *Oliver Cromwell*, *Leander* and *Lord Nelson* coming together we really fulfilled our main-line double-track image."

Tornado was then taken by road to the National Railway Museum for three 75mph test runs on the main line.

However, on October 26, 2013, DB Schenker driver Dave Court – addressing a public gathering at the start of the NRM's Autumn Great Gathering of all six surviving LNER A4 Pacifics – confessed to twice taking *Tornado* up to 90mph during its final test run from Newcastle-on-Tyne to York on November 18, 2008. He was suspended for speeding.

Tornado storms out of Loughborough Central during its return visit in British Railways apple green livery in March 2010. BRIAN SHARPE

Little and large: LMS 'Jinty' 0-6-0T No. 47406 passes No. 60163 at Loughborough on March 21, 2010. ALAN WEAVER/A1 TRUST

It was *Tornado's* last run in grey primer. Back at the NRM, it was painted into LNER apple green livery with British Railways on the tender, as worn by the original locomotives in 1948.

Approved for main line passenger operation, on January 31, 2009, *Tornado* hauled its first passenger trip on the main line – 'The Peppercorn Pioneer' – from York to Newcastle and back, as crowds of enthusiasts and non-enthusiasts alike packed station platforms and vantage points along the route.

Everyone was eager to glimpse this new steam celebrity: teenage girls with mobile telephone cameras jostled with hardcore linesiders for pole positions. Years later, crowds still flock to watch *Tornado* wherever it goes.

Tornado was named by the Prince of Wales and the Duchess of Cornwall at York station on February 19, 2009, before the loco hauled The Royal Train to Leeds.

It was a fairytale ending – and beginning – for the team which had defied the critics to make it happen. Many adventures awaited it on the main line.

In March 2010, *Tornado* returned to the GCR, this time fully painted, as a thank you gesture for those key weeks of initial testing. While builder and owner The A1 Steam Locomotive Trust had otherwise banned moving No. 60163 by road to hire destinations, a rare exception was made for the GCR as it was not rail connected.

A legend had been born – and a line which has become legendary in its own right played a major part. ∎

New-build Peppercorn A1 Pacific No. 60163 *Tornado* makes one of its last runs in grey primer on the Great Central Railway on October 12, 2008. DAVE RODGERS

The third Great Central

We have already seen how the London Extension was dismembered in the wake of the Beeching report, with the Nottingham Arkwright Street to Rugby Central section closing in 1969.

When the Main Line Preservation Group was formed, a large part of the track was still in place, as retold in Chapter 9, allowing the revivalists to acquire a short section running south from Loughborough for a new Great Central.

Founder members dreamed of eventually extending steam services to form an inter-city heritage railway between Nottingham and Leicester. The stated aim from the outset was to preserve the remaining section of the line: however, it quickly became clear that it would be impossible to return to either city centre.

The key word here is "dreamed": for after the dismemberment resumed in 1980, that is surely all it could and would ever be.

The GCR main line to the north of Loughborough had remained in use for freight traffic. A single track was left in situ to serve the British Gypsum works at Rushcliffe and a Ministry of Defence depot at Ruddington, trains initially arriving from Nottingham via Weekday Cross Junction.

The section of the London Extension north of Loughborough had by then been connected by British Rail to the Midland Main Line by the building of a spur line to a new Loughborough East (GC) Junction, commonly referred to today as Loughborough South Junction, in late 1973. Once this chord was open, it was used by the gypsum trains and army depot traffic, and the GC main line from and including Ruddington

station to the north was closed and lifted, while the line to Ruddington and the depot became known as the East Leake branch.

Because of the colossal amount of money involved in an inter-city revival, the preservationists first focused on the section south of Loughborough, in the belief that the surviving section to the north would be safe while it remained in traffic, at least for the time being.

However, in 1980, British Rail removed the bridge which carried the London Extension over the Midland Main Line at Loughborough. Worse still, the embankment and smaller bridges leading to the main bridge were also removed. As far as rail reinstatement from Loughborough to Nottingham was concerned, it seemed an ultimate act of finality.

One of the earliest ex-main line locomotives to be associated with the GCR(N) was LNER Y7 0-4-0T No. 680088, seen shunting at Loughborough Central during a 'southern visit' in 1993. BRIAN SHARPE

The official opening of the extension to 50 Steps Bridge was performed by former Conservative cabinet minister Ken Clarke on June 30, 1995. PHIL SHARPE/GCR(N)

Castle Donington Power Station No. 2 runs to Cripps Bridge following official opening in June 1995. GCR(N)

Left: One of the immortal images of the original Great Central Railway was the viaducts carrying the line above the River Soar in the heart of Leicester. Sadly, that section has been lost to preservation, but Loughborough viaduct has all the ingredients to become one of the definitive photographic locations on Britain's heritage railways. On February 22, 2004, visiting North Norfolk Railway-based GER J15 0-6-0 No. 65462 heads a freight photographic charter over the viaduct, below which the River Soar divides Leicestershire from Nottinghamshire. GEOFF SILCOCK

RUDDINGTON ORDNANCE & SUPPLY DEPOT

The whole story here, however, begins not in 1980, but four decades earlier.

In 1940, the Ministry of Defence bought farmland to the south of Ruddington for a Royal Ordnance Factory for the supply of ammunition as part of the war effort.

It was planned as a filling factory for ammunition, employing up to 4000 people. Such sites were selected because they were away from main centres of population but still accessible by rail, to allow easy access by workers.

The site was levelled off in December 1940 so the factory, named ROF Ruddington; Filling Factory No. 14, could be built, and at the peak of its construction, tens of thousands of labourers were engaged.

The site had more than 200 buildings, and was linked to the London Extension by a freight spur just over a mile long from Ruddington station, facilitating easy access inwards for raw materials as well as quick and safe distribution of the final products.

Half of the site was developed as a separate armaments storage facility.

Gunpowder and shells were ferried in via the freight spur, with trains being marshalled into two different sets of sidings. The components were brought together in the filling halls, some in the heart of the complex, each with their own blast wall.

Completed shells were then moved out to a small storage facility, before being taken out by rail, or by road to local Army or Home Guard units.

The largely self-sufficient site was equipped

with two underground reservoirs, a heating and sewage plant, generators, a telephone exchange, two canteens, a doctors' surgery, a bakery, a laundry and a mortuary.

The entire site was under tight security, with both on-site security staff and military police providing round the clock protection. On Ordnance Survey maps, it appeared as a blank white space, as was the rule regarding military installations that was relaxed only in the 1970s.

The site was decommissioned in 1945, but used by the MoD for army surplus equipment and vehicles, with public auctions taking place every eight weeks. The site was finally closed in 1983.

June 9, 1984 witnessed the last train to the Ruddington depot under British Rail, 'The Ruddington Requiem' diesel multiple unit charter.

The last train to the British Gypsum works ran in 1985. Afterwards the line was, thankfully, left in situ, rather than being ripped up within weeks as had been the policy up to a handful of years before.

In the mid-1980s, it was at first planned to use the depot site for housing, but Nottinghamshire County Council objected.

The site was split into three parts, one being redeveloped in 1990 at a cost of £3.5 million as the 285 acre Rushcliffe Country Park, and the eastern portion becoming a business park.

However, the freight spur and sidings were subsequently redeveloped as the Nottingham Transport Heritage Centre.

THE REVIVALISTS MOVE IN

It was clear from the outset that the missing bridge would be an Everest to climb if the vision of an inter-city heritage railway would ever be realised, but if the line between Loughborough South Junction and Ruddington depot was lifted, revival would be far too big an ask.

And the East Leake branch was certainly a line worth saving, if only for the spectacular brick-built Loughborough viaduct (often referred to as Stamford viaduct) spanning the River Soar, and East Leake or Barnston Tunnel at the line's summit.

In October 1989, the first meeting of the Great Central Railway-Northern Development Association – a new organisation formed by members of the Main Line Steam Trust Nottingham Area Group – was held, and two months later members were allowed access to the mothballed army depot to recover useful materials from old buildings.

The group's initial aim was to lease the MoD depot and 2.77 miles of GCR main line from Fifty Steps Bridge to north of Hotchley Hill signalbox.

In Easter 1990, the Great Central Railway (Nottingham) was officially formed, to save the line from the depot to Loughborough via Ruddington station, one of those closed in 1963.

While demolition of the depot buildings proceeded, the proposed heritage transport collection building was saved. In autumn that year, full access was given to the 11 acre Nottingham Transport Heritage Centre side and vintage buses arrived to start the road transport collection which has been built up there. Also, members recovered Neasden South Junction signalbox for eventual re-erection at the centre.

In 1991, the Nottingham Society of Model & Experimental Engineers arrived. Derelict land grants were obtained to landscape the site and

refurbish the roofs and cladding on each of the four main buildings left after demolition.

The following year, the first industrial diesel locomotives were acquired for shunting, and track laid from the heritage centre to Asher Lane. The first steam locomotive on site was Hudswell Clarke 0-6-0ST No. 1682 of 1937 No. 54 *Julia*, which worked at the British Sugar Corporation plant at Kelham and was first preserved in the Millgate Museum at Newark-on-Trent.

In 1993, the first track was laid into the main locomotive building, and during the August Bank Holiday weekend, the GCR(N) held its first public open days. Robert Stephenson & Hawthorns 0-4-0ST No. 7818 of 1954 *Castle Donington Power Station No.2* provided runpasts.

On September 10, 1993, the official opening of Nottingham Transport Heritage Centre was performed by David Clarke, the longtime GCR supporter and benefactor. For the occasion, LMS Jubilee 4-6-0 No. 5593 4-6-0 *Kolhapur* was borrowed from Birmingham Railway Museum for display, but was not steamed.

The next year saw the first steam-hauled passenger services run from a temporary platform. With ex-Stewarts & Lloyds RSH 0-6-0ST No. 7667 of 1950 No. 56 having been acquired from the now-closed North

Kolhapur prepared and ready for the official opening of the Nottingham Transport /Heritage Centre in the early morning light of September 10, 1993. GCR(N)

Visiting LNER B1 4-6-0 No. 61264 heads a passenger train south from East Leake Tunnel towards Loughborough. B1s would have once been a frequent sight on the London Extension. ROBIN JONES

A motorist's eye view of the first steam train back into Loughborough from the north coming to a halt above the A60 on April 21, 2001. ROBIN JONES

Steam returned to Loughborough from the north on April 21, 2001, with ex-West Somerset Railway preservation pioneer Bagnall 0-6-0ST *Victor* heading an inspection train across Loughborough viaduct, paving the way for many more to follow in the years ahead. ROBIN JONES

Woolwich Station Museum, along with two British Rail Mk.2 coaches, which were immediately vandalised. One of them was refurbished for passenger push-pull working to the level crossing.

The whole of the line from the new heritage centre to a railbreak dividing the GCR(N) from the national network at Bunny Lane on Gotham Moor was acquired, and work began on building a new locomotive shed at the depot. Neasden South signalbox was brought to the site and work started on its reassembly, while the first road transport gala was held at the end of season in October.

In March 1995, track was recovered from Drakelow Power Station. The running line was extended to Bridge 299, also known as 50 Steps Bridge. Ruddington Junction with the GCR main line was reinstated. In June 1995, the GCR(N) ran its first passenger train across an original GC level crossing.

The official opening of the extension to 50 Steps Bridge was performed by Rushliffe MP, Ken Clarke, the former Conservative cabinet minister and occasional GC locomotive driver, on June 30, the day after the Transport & Works Order came into force from the depot as far as the railbreak. A members' train also ran over half a mile of the old main line, its first steam presence since the late 1960s.

In July, HM Railway Inspectorate gave the green light for works trains to run to Rushcliffe Halt, and the following month, a steam crane arrived from the Dean Forest Railway.

The first enthusiast steam photographic charters were run as far as the railbreak in 1996.

In 1998, loans from English, Welsh & Scottish Railway and a local businessman allowed the GCR main line south to Loughborough South Junction to be restored for working trains, and on December 1, the first commercial train worked the route since it was closed in 1983, in the form of desulphogypsum transported from Drax Power Station in Yorkshire to the British Gypsum works at East Leake. For the purpose, a new loading pad constructed on potential GCR(N) land at Rushcliffe Halt.

On October 15, 1999, the first public passenger steam trains ran from the heritage centre to the site of Gotham sidings, a distance of three miles. Furthermore, special dispensation from HM Railway Inspectorate allowed an extended trip into Rushcliffe Halt on June 10 in conjunction with an open day at the adjacent gypsum works, with on-loan LMS Stanier 8F No. 48305, visiting from the southern GCR at Loughborough, hauling the first GCR(N) passenger trains to Rushcliffe during the event.

That autumn, a new charity, the LNER(GC) Heritage Trust was formed. The following year, another new charity, the GCR Rolling Stock Trust, gathered all the GCR Barnum carriages on both heritage lines together at Ruddington.

Following a general boiler overhaul, the Midland & Great Northern Joint Railway Society's visiting flagship B12 4-6-0 No. 61572 returned to traffic on the Great Central Railway (Nottingham) over the weekend of May 19-20, 2001. It is seen calling at Rushcliffe Halt with the 'Master Cutler' on June 3. JOHN BAGSHAW/ GCR(N).

The biggest display of Great Central Railway locomotive nameplates seen since the Grouping of 1923 was staged at the Nottingham Transport Heritage Centre on June 3, 2001. JOHN BAGSHAW/ GCR(N).

Above: Robinson O4 No. 63601 heads towards Ruddington on November 2, 2007, during a visit to the Great Central Railway (Nottingham). BRIAN SHARPE

This EWS gypsum train awaiting unloading at Rushcliffe Halt on July 21, 2000 comprised 41 container wagons – which otherwise would have needed to be taken to the adjacent works by road. If Great Central Railway (Nottingham) revivalists had not reopened the line, scores of heavy lorries would be trundling through the village of East Leake on a daily basis. ROBIN JONES

All ours! History was in the making: Railtrack Midland Zone director Richard Fearn (left) hands over the deeds of the Loughborough-Hotchley Hill line to then Great Central Railway (Nottingham) director Tony Sparks at Rushcliffe Halt on June 3, 2001. JOHN BAGSHAW/GCR(N).

TAKING FULL OWNERSHIP

In 1998, contracts were drawn up for the GCR(N) to buy the 5½ miles of the GCR main line from Hotchley Hill sidings, just past Rushcliffe Halt to the point where the spur leads to Loughborough South Junction.

By then, the heritage line already owned the 3¾miles of track on the former Great Central main line running north to Fifty Steps Bridge and the depot spur.

Under the terms of the £200,000 sale, the GCR(N) had to allow EWS free access to run midweek freight trains to the British Gypsum factory at Hotchley Hill, and also refurbish the line to Railtrack standards. In return, EWS provided a quarter of the purchase price, which was to be paid in instalments over the next three years.

Contractors were hired by the GCR(N) that October to carry out essential remedial and upgrading work to the new line.

Trackwork Ltd., of Doncaster relaid the mile-long stretch from the Stanford Road overbridge to the site of the old lime siding south of the 98 yard East Leake Tunnel.

February 9, 2001 saw Freightliner Class 66 No. 66511 headed a train of 10 Autoballasters in Railtrack livery from the Midland Main Line on to the GCR(N) for training sessions in operating the high-tech radio-controlled ballast wagons. It comprised the first 'real' freight train into Ruddington for nearly 20 years.

Making several low-speed passes, the train deposited about 200 tons of material in the area south of Gotham sidings for plain line work, after which the train ran on to Fifty Steps Bridge and along the spur into the heritage centre.

There, it dropped a further 60 tons on to recently-laid station throat pointwork. Arriving on to GCR(N) metals at about 2.30pm, the train stayed until nearly 8pm, giving the trainees experience of both

daylight and darkness situations.

The joint exercise with Railtrack and Freightliner was considered to be a success, and from that eight further sessions were immediately organised.

Subsequent to the Autoballaster trials it had been hoped that Railtrack, and later Network Rail, would increase their visits to the line. However, one of the legacies of the British Rail lifting of the second track was the signalling system. This hampered the revivalists, limiting the use of the line to a one engine in steam operation.

While training sessions over the years encouraged ballast cleaners and tampers and even the Long Welded Rail train to check out systems and crews, there were regular on-track training sessions for permanent-way workers and a number of graduate familiarisation courses for foundation students from Sheffield Hallam University, among others.

The GCR(N) plant event had a demonstration of one of the first uses of laser control of ballast levelling in the country, bringing precision of a specially fitted Laser dozer to Platform No. 2 at the centre.

One fascinating problem facing the present-GCRN that kept on occurring was at the earthworks related to the line's original construction in the late 1890s. This was where two main contractors met, just north of East Leake Tunnel.

Here in recent years the ground swelled in the wet, shrank in the dry and the wet. The track slewed and distorted continuously.

The nearby-based British Geological Survey set up a satellite controlled monitoring system on site to uncover what weather conditions were the cause and indeed the actual effect, researching right back to the tipping methods and materials that were employed by contractor Henry Lovatt. The latter revealed that despite a massive cutting

Victor and its short inspection train pass the as-yet-unrestored Hotchley Hill signalbox on April 21, 2001. ROBIN JONES

at East Leake (the largest on the London Extension) there was no spare spoil from the next contractor, Logan & Hemingway, and all sorts of mixed materials were used to form the high embankment.

Trees allowed by BR to grow into the embankment merely added to the more recent problems. A substantial corrective track relaying and drainage modifying plan was a requirement.

Bogged down by persistent legal delays, the purchase deal had taken at least three years to go through. Its completion on March 31, 2001 opened the door the GCR(N) to proceed with plans to run its own weekend heritage trains to Loughborough, initially the northern side of the missing bridge.

RETURNING TO LOUGHBOROUGH

Saturday, April 21, 2001 saw the first steam train run down the line to Loughborough since 1967.

An inspection train, comprising recent arrival Bagnall 0-6-0ST No. 2996 of 1950 *Victor*, two five-plank wagons and two brakevans, ran from the heritage centre base at Ruddington to a point just beyond the A60 bridge on the outskirts of the town, opposite the Brush locomotive works.

Not only did the train carry members of the GCR(N)'s permanent way gang but Railtrack inspectors who needed to satisfy themselves about future arrangements for access to the line, as it still comes under the control of

Leicester power signalbox.

The short train was hugely symbolic in more ways than one. For *Victor* was one of the two former Longbridge, Birmingham car plant Bagnalls which helped launch the debut services on the West Somerset Railway 25 years before. History was repeating itself as it paved the way for regular steam passenger services into Loughborough from the north.

Ironically, it was the GCR at Loughborough which celebrated its 25th anniversary as a company just over a fortnight later, on May 9.

The train departed from the heritage centre shortly after 10am, reversing up the depot spur to gain the GCR main line.

Arriving at the derelict but eminently restorable Hotchley Hill signalbox, the train

Roger Hibbert's LMS Stanier 8F No. 48305, which is based at Loughborough shed, hauled the Great Central Railway (Nottingham)'s first public passenger steam train to Rushcliffe Halt on June 10, 2000. SIMON V HOPKINS

On June 30, 1995, Ken Clarke MP, watched by GCR(N) chairman Peter J Ward, opens the temporary three-carriage platform at the heritage centre. PHIL SHARPE/GCR(N)

paused briefly to obtain permission to enter the section which had just been acquired by the GCR(N), and a few moments later it pulled into Rushcliffe Halt witnessed by a crowd of spectators on the overbridge.

Eventually the green flag was waved to allow *Victor* to break new ground in preservation by heading south. At both East Leake Tunnel and Loughborough viaduct, several runpasts were made for the benefit of lineside photographers.

Grinding to a halt after crossing the A60, the stop at Loughborough brought the traffic on the road below to a halt, and a prolonged blast on the whistle proclaimed the GCR(N)'s arrival into the town.

The sound carried southwards in the wind and was acknowledged by the locomotives in Loughborough Central station. A few passing High Speed Trains and Turbos on the Midland Main Line added their greeting.

Victor, its BR-style lined black livery gleaming in the sunshine, then edged right down to the actual boundary line and photographs were taken of the historic occasion. Care was taken, however, to ensure

that the train did not over run and set off the track circuit in the signalbox. Being sequential locking, it would have seized up the main line!

The train stood in front of the spur of overgrown embankment in front of the missing bridge.

THE RETURN OF THE FAYS

The purchase of the line immediately led to photographic charters by visiting locomotives running all the way to Loughborough becoming a regular occurrence, while the first special passenger trains to Rushcliffe Halt and then Loughborough from the Nottingham Transport Heritage Centre were run.

On June 3, 2001, the GCR(N) celebrated a decade of progress since the first volunteers began work on the heritage centre.

Hauled by visiting LNER B12 4-6-0 No. 61572, a version of 'The Master Cutler' stopped at Rushcliffe Halt, probably for the first time ever.

Richard Fearn, Railtrack's Midland Zone director, stepped from the train driven by Great Central Railway Society president Richard Hardy to present the deeds of the line

and a commemorative plaque to GCR(N) director Tony Sparks, record the purchase on March 31, and for the first time in more than 75 years, 38 original GCR locomotive nameplates were shown again in public.

Sir Sam Fay's son Edgar Fay, by then in his nineties, climbed into a brand new Caterpillar backhoe loader supplied by railway plant specialist Sinbad of Nottingham, to ceremonially turn the first turf of the heritage centre's new No. 4 building.

Neasden South Junction signalbox, now re-erected at the heritage centre terminus, was also used for the first time.

Sir Sam's grandson John Fay, a society vice president, pulled off the home starter to send the train under way, bringing a cacophony of blasts from the Class 20 D8048 as it opened up on its way out, its rake of coaches topped and tailed by the B12.

The pair then ran a special hourly four-coach passenger service to Rushcliffe Halt.

To celebrate the event, two special ales were brewed, Sir Sam Fay's Commemorative Ale and the Sheffield Special Real Ale, both by Castle Rock Brewery of Nottingham. Both

Visiting LBSCR 'Terrier' 0-6-0T No. 662 *Martello* approaches Bridge 300 during its short stay on the Great Central Railway (Nottingham) in May 2011. RUDDINGTONRSH56*

Robert Stephenson & Hawthorns 'Ugly' class 0-6-0ST No. 56, a staple performer on the Great Central Railway (Nottingham) prepares to depart Ruddington Fields with a passenger working in May 2009. After withdrawal from Stewarts & Lloyds service in 1969, this locomotive's first home in preservation was at the Kent and East Sussex Railway, operating there briefly in the Seventies. THOMAS H-TAYLOR*

Visiting GWR 4-4-0 No. 3440 *City of Truro*, unofficially the first steam locomotive in the world to top 100mph, pulls away from 50 Steps Bridge with a December 2010 Santa special service. RUDDINGTONRSH56*

Visiting NER J72 0-6-0T No. 69023 *Joem* heads towards Bridge 300 during the 2011 Santa specials. RUDDINGTONRSH56*

GWR 4-6-0 No. 4965 *Rood Ashton Hall* makes heritage era history as it brings the first main line steam excursion on to the Great Central Railway (Nottingham) on November 22, 2003. It is seen climbing up the curve from the junction with the Midland Main Line. JOHN BAGSHAW

were tasted by Edgar and son John Fay who gave their approval.

More history was made at Loughborough when the GCR(N) ran its first passenger train to the town from the north. EWS Class 37 No. 37667 *Meldon Quarry Centenary*, visiting the heritage centre for its July 28/29 diesel gala, stopped opposite Brush locomotive works.

In 2002, there was periodic working between the centre and Rushcliffe Halt, while a large influx of money came from a cable company for access along the line.

That winter, Rushcliffe Halt station was brought back into service.

The August bank holiday weekend of 2003 saw the GCR(N) revivalists stage celebrations to mark the 10th anniversary of their first open day. GB Railfreight Class 66 No. 66707 was officially named *Sir Sam Fay-Great Central Railway*, while the new platforms at the heritage centre were started, and the topping-out ceremony for the roof on the new locomotive shed was held.

The heritage centre received its first return steam special from the main line on November 22, 2003, behind Tyseley-based GWR 4-6-0 No. 4965 *Rood Ashton Hall*. The Vintage Trains charter ran from Tyseley Warwick Road via Water Orton, Nuneaton and Leicester to Ruddington. The GCR(N) may have been years behind its southern Great Central heritage counterpart, but unlike it, has been able to enjoy the benefits of a main line connection.

In 2005, the London & North Eastern Railway Company formed as the main holding company for the northern GCR operation,

while Nottingham Transport Heritage Centre Ltd and Great Central Railway (Nottingham) Ltd became operating companies.

Ruddington Fields is the name given to the station at the Nottingham Transport Heritage Centre, distinguishing it from the original Ruddington station. The new platforms there were opened in 2009.

One station that has not been reopened is East Leake, mainly due to lack of car parking, and with the entrance being directly onto the road under the bridge. The station buildings have been demolished, with the rubble used to fill in the area from the road entrance to the platform. The island platform remains in place, but a small goods siding next to the station was redeveloped for housing in the 1990s.

One station that has not been reopened is East Leake, mainly due to lack of car parking, and with the entrance being directly onto the road under the bridge. The station buildings have been demolished, with the rubble used to fill in the area from the road entrance to the platform. The island platform remains in place, but the goods yard next to the station was redeveloped for housing in the 1990s.

RUDDINGTON STATION

The original Ruddington station was on the western side of the village and was of typical Great Central island platform style, accessed by stairs from an entrance in the centre of the bridge spanning the line at the north end of the station.

It was somewhat similar in design to Quorn & Woodhouse with a similar road over

bridge type and goods yard size. The booking office was on the platform. The centre piers of the bridge were left hollow to provide lamp rooms.

In original Great Central days, 17 trains in each direction stopped there each day. The station was closed on March 4, 1963, but stayed open for goods until May 1, 1967.

The buildings have all been demolished, leaving just the platforms, fenced off from the GCR(N), heavily overgrown and now surrounded by housing.

Developer Crest Homes was twice refused planning permission by Rushcliffe Borough Council for homes on the site. However, a compromise was eventually reached, whereby development was allowed on the goods yard, but leaving a narrow strip of land on the formation of the main line for the future extension of GCR(N) services when the time is right.

In 2010 the island platform and sufficient room for tracks to pass either side by bought from British Railways Board (residuary) by the GCR(N)'s supporting charity the East Midlands Railway Trust, along with around 300 yards of trackbed to the north.

In the future, it is hoped to restore it for heritage railway use, with a relaid line maybe running on to a new interchange with an extension to the modern-day Nottingham light rail tram system (see Chapter 18). If that and other major developments happen, it may well be possible to travel again over the London Extension from the outskirts of Leicester into Nottingham city centre.

Waiting for the trains to return: the overgrown site of Ruddington station on the London Extension, now owned by a charitable trust but hemmed in by modern housing. Very much one for the future. RICHARD VINCE *

Resident RSH 'Ugly' class 0-6-0ST No. 63 *Corby* stands at Ruddington Fields station in December 2011. Withdrawn from service in 1969 from Stewarts & Lloyds in Corby, it was preserved on the Keighley & Worth Valley Railway where it briefly worked in the Eighties. Unlike its southern counterpart, the Great Central Railway (Nottingham) still relies on industrial types for passenger trains. RUDDINGTONRSH56 *

THE 'SCREAMING VALENTA'

On November 15, 2014, the GCR(N) was in the heritage sector spotlight, when the National Railway Museum's prototype High Speed Train power car No. 410001 made its first passenger-carrying run in preservation at the head of a Class 125 inter-city unit.

The 'Screaming Valenta', as the landmark special from Ruddington Fields to the north of Loughborough was titled, followed the three-year restoration to running order of the power car by the 125 Group Project Miller team, in association with the NRM.

On May 31, 2014, No. 41001 completed a loaded test run along the GCR(N) hauling two Mk.2 carriages and a Class 56 locomotive, but the special was its first passenger train since 1976. The fundraising special started its journey as a regular East Midlands Trains production High Speed Train, shortened at Etches Park Depot from the normal eight coaches to only six, with power cars Nos. 43045 and 43054 at either end of the set. Starting from Derby at 10.25am, also picking up at Loughborough, the train conveyed invited guests, supporters and 125 Group members.

Also on board was special guest Sir Kenneth Grange, who designed the iconic shape of the prototype and production HSTs and is also honorary president of the 125 Group. At Loughborough South Junction, the special crossed onto the GCR(N), over the spur which remains in Network Rail ownership for now. At Ruddington Fields, shunting took place and No. 41001 replaced production power car 43045 on the set. Following speeches from Sir Kenneth and senior railway figures and a champagne toast, passengers reboarded for the maiden journey.

The hybrid HST then departed from Ruddington Fields, with the power cars running in full multiple operation, both powering the train. Following reversal at Fifty Steps Bridge, No. 41001 led the train on a storming run up the London Extension to the site of the GCR(N)'s proposed Loughborough High Level station, stopping at Rushcliffe Halt for photographs to be taken.

The train then returned north with No. 41001 at the rear, still providing traction power. At Ruddington Fields, the power cars were swapped back and the train returned to Leicester, Loughborough and Derby, bringing to a close a truly historic day. Class 125 units have arguably been the most successful forms of traction in the history of Britain's railways, having been in service for four decades, and no end in sight.

In the early 1970s the British Railways decided to replace its main-line express diesel traction. Mass electrification was deemed too costly, so a new generation of high-speed diesel trains had to be developed.

Experience with the high-speed Class 55 Deltics had shown that a low axle weight was essential to avoid damage to the track at sustained high speed, and that high-speed engines were the only way to provide a good enough power/weight ratio for diesels.

To power the proposed High Speed Trains at up to 125mph (201kph), each power car had a new diesel engine, the 12-cylinder Paxman Valenta, capable of 2250 horsepower.

The two prototype power cars, Nos. 41001/2 were developed at the Railway Technical

With the cooling towers of Ratcliffe-on-Soar Power Station in the distance, West Country light Pacific No. 34007 *Wadebridge*, visiting from the Mid Hants Railway, heads north from East Leake Tunnel back to Ruddington Fields on May 3, 2013. GRAHAM KEMP

History in the making on the Great Central Railway (Nottingham) yet again: High Speed Train prototype power car No. 41001 heads an East Midlands Class 125 away from Ruddington Fields station on November 14, 2014. BRIAN SHARPE

Centre in Derby and appeared in 1972. After proving trials on the Eastern Region the prototype train was used Paddington to Bristol/Weston-super-Mare services.

The design was successful and led to production orders being placed for similar trains for the Western, Eastern, Scottish and London Midland Regions.

The class is the fastest diesel locomotive in the world, with a maximum speed of 148mph and a regular service speed of 125mph.

The November 14 run was also the first time that a Paxman Valenta has powered a passenger train since this engine type was withdrawn from main line use in 2010.

So history was made on several fronts on the day – and it will not be the last time that happens on the Great Central Railway (Nottingham). ■

Class 20 No. 20007 heads a Great Central Railway (Nottingham) service. The line has built up a sizeable fleet of heritage diesels over the years. GRAHAM KEMP

Visiting Bulleid West Country light Pacific No. 34007 *Wadebridge* and BR Standard 2MT 2-6-0 No. 78019 from Loughborough shed top and tail a passenger service over Loughborough Viaduct on May 4, 2013. GRAHAM KEMP

A crowd gathers on the Ruddington Fields platform as High Speed Train prototype power car No. 41001 prepares to head a production Class 125 set to Loughborough on November 14, 2014. ALEX HARGRAVES

CHAPTER 15

GREAT LOCOS, GREAT GALAS, GREAT CENTRAL

Boscastle's sister Bulleid West Country light Pacific No. 34101 *Hartland*, based on the North Yorkshire Moors Railway, is seen at Swithland on February 25, 1995. BRIAN SHARPE

Although it was built late in the day, the original Great Central Railway with its fast route into the heart of London was, in many ways, a masterpiece.

Exactly the same can be said about today's Great Central, which occupies just an eight-mile section of the London Extension.

Since the volunteer-led preservation movement began with the saving of the Talyllyn Railway in 1951, Britain now has a proud portfolio of more than 120 operating heritage railways.

They all have much to commend them in their own right.

However, here is something that is truly different – a preserved section of a reborn double-track trunk route, and one which acts like it is.

When I first visited the revived GCR as it began to seriously take shape, what struck me most of all was not the locomotive fleet or

rolling stock, but the 'naturalness' of the stations and infrastructure.

Many of our heritage railways have recreated some wonderful picture-postcard settings and cameo scenes airbrushed to perfection, but the Great Central is different.

Having grown up with steam railways from an early age in a Midland town – my elder brother Stewart regularly took me trainspotting the school holidays in the early Sixties – here was something with which I could truly identify. Loughborough Central, Quorn & Woodhouse and Rothley – they were just like the stations in everyday use I had passed through on the steam age with no tourist embellishments or added ornamentation.

I still feel that way about the GCR, and in this respect, it is a true time warp in the purest sense of the phrase, a raw recreation of what was, not an idealistic version seen through rose-tinted spectacles.

Why do more heritage lines not follow this example and leave telegraph poles in place at strategic photographic locations such as Kinchley Lane, for instance? In the past, telegraph poles were to be found along every stretch of railway, so why is this small detail missing from other lines today?

The Main Line Steam Trust set out to recreate a typical section of a trunk route as it existed in the final decades of steam, when first-generation diesels appeared. The march it has stolen on other heritage railways is not just because of fine details such as telegraph poles, but the fact it is the world's only double-track line of its type.

As yet, it is not possible to run a complete original GCR train over it. That will happen someday in the future, but architecture apart, there are few similarities with the pre-Grouping company. What today's GCR has become is a magnificent stage over which it is possible to run any main line locomotive, steam or diesel,

LNER A4 Pacific No. 60007 *Sir Nigel Gresley* viewed from Kinchley Lane during a visit in 1993. BRIAN SHARPE.

THE LINE FOR ALL SEASONS

Full fathom five thy father lies;
Of his bones are coral made;
Those are pearls that were
his eyes;
Nothing of him that doth fade,
But doth suffer a sea-change
Into something rich and
strange.

William Shakespeare,
The Tempest

Above: LNER D49 4-4-0 No. 62712 *Morayshire* had visited the GCR from its Bo'ness & Kinneil Railway home before, but in its long-time heritage-era livery of LNER apple green as LNER No. 246. However, 2014 saw a briefly change to the 'enthusiast's choice' of BR black, and the only line south of the border to hire it in the livery was GCR. As No. 62712, it is seen heading a TPO train out of Loughborough Central during the autumn steam gala. JULIE RODGERS

in a truly evocative setting, whether historically appropriate to any of the six decades when the London extension was in use or not, for the benefit of visitors, or as a perfect setting for location filming of a big-screen or TV drama.

Trains passing on a double-track main line, express passenger workings passing a 'windcutter' freight, a Travelling Post Office set, which really does collect the mail, and a wonderful home fleet of both steam and heritage diesel traction, with more restoration projects in the offing.

This chapter is a celebration of that fleet, and some of the many classic visiting locomotives that have run over the line; a contrast from the Robinson era as described in Chapter 3, but one that can easily stand head and shoulders alongside its Edwardian predecessors.

Indeed, it begins to read like a Who's Who of the finest of Britain's surviving steam locomotives.

WR Modified Hall 4-6-0 No. 6990 *Witherslack Hall* at Woodthorpe on April 19, 1987. BRIAN SHARPE

Sir Lamiel passes snowbound Woodthorpe with the 9am from Loughborough on January 26, 2014. ALAN CORFIELD

SIR LAMIEL, THE SCOTCH ARTHUR

Part of the National Collection, but based on the GCR, is Southern Railway N15 King Arthur class 4-6-0 *Sir Lamiel*.

Supplied by the North British Locomotive Company in June 1925, it was one of the last batches of N15s, known as 'Scotch Arthurs' because they were built in Glasgow.

The N15s were introduced by Robert Urie, LSWR chief mechanical engineer, in 1919 and were initially very successful, but they suffered from poor steaming capabilities and in 1925, Southern Railway CME Richard Maunsell modified class members. Initially numbered E777, *Sir Lamiel* was first allocated to Nine Elms shed to haul expresses from Waterloo station to the West Country and Bournemouth.

Withdrawn from service in October 1961, it was first stored at Fratton, then Stratford and Ashford. In June 1978 it was adopted by the Humberside Locomotive Preservation Group and taken to its base at Dairycoates shed in Hull, where it was restored to main line standard.

It steamed there on February 21, 1982 and on March 27 made its first trip over the Settle & Carlisle line. It has since made numerous forays on the main line in the heritage era.

Following repairs at Tyseley Locomotive and Loughborough in October 2012, it emerged in Southern Railway malachite green livery as No. 777 for the first time having previously carried SR olive green with that number and in British Railways Brunswick green as No. 30777 in preservation.

LMS 'BLACK FIVE' NO. 45305

It is not only Dai Woodham at Barry who is celebrated for enabling scrap main line steam locomotives to be saved for preservation.

'Black Five' No. 5305 was built by Armstrong-Whitworth of Newcastle-on-Tyne in 1936 and was renumbered 45305 at Nationalisation. Mainly based in north-west England throughout its working life, No. 45305 lasted in service until the last month of steam on British Railways.

It was due to take part in the final main line steam train run by BR, the fabled 'Fifteen Guinea Special' of August 11, 1968, but was failed with a collapsed firebox brick arch the night before and was replaced by sister engine No. 45110, which ended up on the Severn Valley Railway.

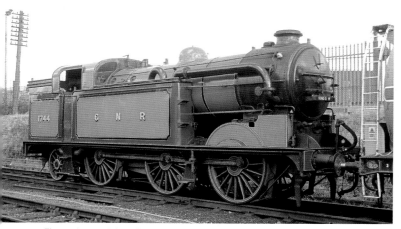

The sole-surviving Gresley N2 0-6-2T in its livery as Great Northern Railway No. 1744, a King's Cross engine. ROBIN JONES

LMS Stanier 'Black Five' 4-6-0 No. 45305 stands at Loughborough Central on July 17, 2002, long before the canopy was renewed in a £450,000 three-year project. Notice the difference! ROBIN JONES

Right: In the autumn of 2011, a fully working 60ft turntable was installed at Quorn & Woodhouse station, the GCR offloading post for visiting locomotives. Not only a visitor attraction in its own right, especially on gala days, it allows locomotives to be turned to run in opposite directions smokebox first, doubling the opportunities available for lineside photographers. The turntable was built in 1909 by Cowans Sheldon Ltd of Carlisle, and was first installed at York shed, since converted into the National Railway Museum. It was acquired in a derelict condition in 2009 and refurbished by GCR engineering staff. Ivatt mogul No. 46521 is seen being turned. GCR

Withdrawn from service at Lostock Hall shed that same month, it was sold to scrap merchant Albert Drapers and Sons Ltd of Hull. The owner of the scrapyard, AE Draper saved the locomotive because it was the cleanest engine in the yard. The locomotive today is managed by the 5305 Locomotive Association. It was restored to its original LMS livery and steamed again in 1976.

In 1984, No. 5305 was named *Alderman AE Draper* by the Mayor of Hedon, Bill Tong. AE Draper was twice Mayor of Hedon and the Hedon coat of arms is on the nameplates, which are not always carried.

It returned to the main line and did much work on specials over the West Highland Line between Fort William and Mallaig. Its boiler certificate ran out in December 1994 and it did not return to traffic until August 2003.

It made its GCR comeback in BR lined black livery with the late crest as No. 45305 following overhaul at Loughborough where it has been based since 1996, and has a current main line certificate.

GRESLEY'S TANK

Sir Nigel Gresley is best known as the designer of the world-beating LNER A3 and A4 Pacifics.

However, he also designed many very good smaller locomotives – not least of all the Great Northern Railway N2 0-6-2Ts that appeared in 1920. They were intended for suburban passenger operations and worked most of the duties out of King's Cross and Moorgate, often hauling one or two Quad-Art sets of articulated suburban coaches, one of which survives on the North Norfolk Railway.

They were also a common sight in and round Glasgow and Edinburgh operating suburban services on the North Clyde Line.

Only one, North British Locomotive Company-built No. 1744 (BR No. 69523) survives in preservation, and while it is based on the Great Central Railway, makes regular visits to other lines. It was one of those class members fitted with condensing apparatus for working on the Metropolitan Railway Widened Lines between King's Cross and Moorgate, that's now part of the London Underground.

After being withdrawn in 1962 from Peterborough's New England depot and now owned by the Gresley Society, it has appeared in LNER and BR black and GNR apple green. Last returned to steam in 2009, it is currently liveried as GNR No. 1744.

Today's heritage steam fleet shows an imbalance towards GWR and Southern types. That's because Barry scrapyard, which held off cutting up locomotives until long after the end of BR steam, until the time the preservation movement had gained sufficient momentum to buy 213 survivors. The location of Woodham Brothers in South Wales meant that it was in pole position to take locomotives from the Western and Southern regions, and that comprised the bulk of its purchases. However, one LNER locomotive was saved from Barry, in the form of Thompson B1 4-6-0 No. 61264.

Built by North British in Glasgow in December 1947, it first entered traffic from Parkeston shed on the Essex coast, working heavy boat trains between Liverpool Street and Harwich. It was transferred to Colwick shed near Nottingham in November 1960 to work all types of passenger and freight duties, including running on the London Extension and the GCR lines to Grimsby and Immingham. Withdrawn in November 1965, it was used as a stationary boiler at Colwick until July 1967, reaching Barry in September 1968. Bought by the Thompson B1 Locomotive Trust, it was taken to the Great Central Railway in July 1976 at Loughborough for the start of a 21-year restoration costing more than £230,000, including extensive boiler work.

On March 6, 1997, it moved under its own power for the first time, three weeks later hauling its first heritage-era passenger train. As LNER No. 1264, it ran at Loughborough for the rest of the season, but in 1998 was moved to Carnforth for main line certification, achieved on March 28 that year with the aid of a Heritage Lottery Fund grant, which helped with the cost of new tyres. In May 1998, No. 1264 was the star of London Underground's Steam on the Met. It worked extensively on the national network and visited heritage railways before withdrawal for a lengthy overhaul in 2008. Having returned to steam at Crewe on October 27, 2012 it is based on the North Yorkshire Moors Railway. It is pictured running over Swithland Reservoir on the GCR in 2002. BRIAN SHARPE

THE RED STANIER 8F

The Great Central has always been great for authenticity endearing it to enthusiasts. However, from time to time, a locomotive may appear in the 'wrong' colours.

Such an example is LMS Stanier 8F No. 8624, which has carried a fictional shade of crimson lake livery since its restoration from ex-Barry condition was completed at Peak Rail in 2009.

It is often said, with much justification, that while the lineside cameramen adore BR black, the 'general public' audience, especially those with young children, love brightly painted engines even more.

Therefore, to paint a black locomotive in a garish colour will horrify the purists, but may well generate a healthy income stream.

Today's heritage railways often have to balance such considerations, because it is impossible to survive on enthusiasm alone, although a volunteer army goes a long way towards that end.

No. 8624 was built at Ashford in December 1943 – indeed, it is the only surviving Southern Railway-built example – it spent its entire working life at Willesden shed in North London, the principal freight depot for the area.

The 8Fs based there worked regularly over the lines to Crewe, Liverpool and Manchester, also to Rugby and Leicester via the Midland route.

As No. 48624, its post-Nationalisation number, it was withdrawn in July 1965, and arrived at Barry that October.

It spent nearly 16 years rusting in the Severn estuary air before it was bought for preservation in July 1981, and taken to Peak Rail's original base at Buxton.

It is now based permanently at the Great Central Railway.

Red-liveried Stanier 8F No. 48624 heads out of Loughborough Central on May 11, 2014.
ROBIN JONES

THE IVATT MOGUL

By contrast to No. 48624, Ivatt 2MT 2-6-0 No. 46521 spent just four years in Barry scrapyard, from March 1967 until it was bought for use on the Severn Valley Railway in March 1971.

Henry George Ivatt, the last chief mechanical engineer of the LMS, produced a modern-looking mogul to replace pre-Grouping 0-6-0 designs, and while they first appeared under the LMS in 1946, British Railways was so impressed with them that it continued to produce them alongside the Standards until 1953. A total of 128 were built.

Further engines of this type were built as the BR Standard 2MT 2-6-0. They had BR standard fittings and a modified cab and tender profile to allow completely unrestricted route availability.

No. 46521 was one of the final batch of 25 Ivatt moguls and appeared from Swindon in February 1953. First based at Brecon, it worked extensively throughout central Wales.

After being bought from Barry by Charles Newton, as the 12th locomotive to be saved from the scrapyard for preservation purposes, it was first steamed in preservation at Bridgnorth in July 1974, and ran in traffic there until 1984. Following overhaul, it steamed on the SVR between 1991 and 2000.

The versatile BR Standard 2MT mogul No. 78019 running light engine at Quorn & Woodhouse.
ROBIN JONES

THE world's most famous steam locomotive, LNER A3 Pacific No. 4472 *Flying Scotsman*, has visited the heritage-era GCR. It is seen in action at Leicester North on January 1, 1993. No. 4472, bought by the National Railway Museum for £2.31 million, is at the time of writing, completing an overhaul which has cost around £3 million, for a return to steam in 2015. BRIAN SHARPE

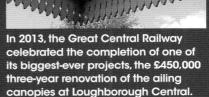

The penultimate member of Stanier's class of LMS moguls to be withdrawn, and the sole example to be preserved, No. 42968 heads towards Kinchley Lane on January 27, 2007, while visiting from its Severn Valley Railway home. ROBIN JONES

Charles Newton, who did not want to see the locomotive take several years to reach the head of the restoration queue again, agreed with the Loughborough Standard Locomotives Group to move it to the GCR.

An extensive and costly rebuild began as soon as the restoration of BR Standard 2MT 2-6-0 No. 78019 was completed, as outlined below. At last, No. 46521 moved under its own power for the first time in almost 11 years shortly before Christmas 2011.

STANDARD MOGUL NO. 78019

Representing the next stage of development of Ivatt's mogul on the GCR is BR Standard 2MT 2-6-0 No. 78019, a popular go-anywhere performer, which has also showed its mettle on several other heritage railways.

The type appeared in 1952, and were so similar to their Ivatt predecessors that the question was often asked whether it was worth the time and trouble in improving the design.

Built at Darlington Works in March 1954, it was first allocated to Kirkby Stephen and worked on local and banking duties through the Lake District. It was later based at Willesden and used to haul empty coaching stock out of Euston.

Withdrawn from Crewe South in November 1966, it ended up at Barry scrapyard.

Also bought by Charles Newton, it left Barry for the Severn Valley Railway in March 1973, and a start was made on restoration in 1980.

Eventually, its owner made a deal with the Loughborough Standard Locomotive Group on the same lines as the later one involving No. 46521, which involved joint ownership.

In 2013, the Great Central Railway celebrated the completion of one of its biggest-ever projects, the £450,000 three-year renovation of the ailing canopies at Loughborough Central.

The 1890s Grade II listed glass, steel and wood canopy, one of the largest station roofs in preservation and known as Loughborough's Crystal Palace, was funded through the GCR's Raising the Roof appeal backed by grants from charitable trusts.

The project was co-ordinated by volunteers, who were also able to refurbish some of the original wooden components. Meanwhile contractors built new steelwork and installed the glass. A total of 860 panes of glass were replaced and more than 1300 new 'dagger boards', which surround the edge of the canopy were manufactured. The end result was not only the saving of the canopy, but allowing more light on to the platforms. Managing director, Bill Ford, said: "The canopy is the defining feature of Loughborough Central. From its sad and sorry state it has been dramatically transformed.

"The canopy will protect generations of future visitors. They'll be able to experience this handsome Victorian town station as intended."

The canopy was declared complete in a special ceremony on August 8, 2013, by Charnwood Borough Council leader, David Slater.

Sufficiently 'dirtied up' to represent the dying days of British Railways' steam, 9F No. 92214 heads a freight train out of Loughborough on May 11, 2014. ROBIN JONES

LNER A2 4-6-2 No. 60532 *Blue Peter* passes Woodthorpe Lane on October 31, 1992. Out of action for most of the 21st century, this popular main line performer, which was adopted by the BBC TV children's programme of the same name, joined multi-millionaire Jeremy Hosking's locomotive fleet and is set for restoration to main line standard. BRIAN SHARPE

In 1998, it moved to Loughborough for a serious restoration to begin, and made its public debut in steam at the GCR summer gala in 2004.

THE GALA GUEST THAT JOINED THE FLEET

No. 92214 visited the Great Central Railway for its January 24-26, 2014 winter steam gala – and ended up not going home again.

GCR director Michael Gregory of Cromwell Tools bought the ex-Barry locomotive from owner Stuart Whitter – and it joined the Loughborough fleet permanently.

The 9F had previously been based at the North Yorkshire Moors Railway, but its latter-day steamings there had been limited.

Stuart, who once was a driver on the GCR, said: "Our experience has given us confidence that No. 92214 will be in the best of hands at GCR."

No. 92214 was built at Swindon in October 1959 and was allocated at Cardiff Canton, Banbury (for ironstone train duties), Newport (Ebbw Junction), Bath Green Park (for holiday excursions over the Somerset & Dorset main line and may have been the last of the class to run over the Mendips), and Severn Tunnel

LMS Stanier 8F 2-8-0 No. 48305 departs from Loughborough during the 2008 winter steam gala. ROBIN JONES

Junction from where it was withdrawn in August 1965.

It arrived at Barry scrapyard that October, and remained until December 1980, when it was bought for restoration by the Peak Railway Society at Buxton. It had spent twice as long in the scrapyard as it had done in BR service. However, it was eventually restored to steam at the Midland Railway-Butterley.

In 2010, No. 92214 moved to the North Yorkshire Moors Railway on loan for the summer, before being bought by Stuart's Grosmont-based company PV Premier Ltd.

It returned to Moors traffic in the summer of 2011, but the following winter needed more extensive repairs and maintenance in order to run the following season.

In 2011, it was named *Cock o' the North*, a name that's been dropped since its arrival at Loughborough. The name, more commonly associated with the first Gresley P2 2-8-2, had been suggested by Valerie Walter, the company secretary of PV Premier Ltd. Her grandfather served with the Gordon Highlanders during the First World War, Cock o' the North being the traditional epithet attached to the chief of the Gordon Clan.

The 9F arrived at the GCR on January 27, 2014, in time for the winter gala, and shortly afterwards it was announced that it had been bought. No. 92214 was subsequently repainted into lined BR Brunswick green as carried by sister No. 92220 *Evening Star*.

THE PRODIGAL 8F

Built at Crewe in November 1943, LMS Stanier 8F 2-8-0 No. 8305 (BR 48305) was first allocated to Leeds, but spent most of its working life in the Midlands.

Switched to Wellingborough in late 1944, it hauled heavy coal trains on the Midland Main Line between Toton and Brent but was, on occasions, also pressed into passenger service.

Later allocated to Crewe South and Northwich, it was withdrawn from Speke Junction in January 1968.

It arrived at Barry in September that year, and while there the words "Please don't let me die!" were sprayed on the smokebox door.

It was Roger Hibbert who rescued the 8F in November 1985, taking it to the GCR for restoration.

Stanier 8Fs, which first appeared in 1935, were once a regular sight on the London

Extension in BR days, and its presence there was entirely in keeping with the revivalists' mission statement to recreate a main line of the Fifties and Sixties. The 8F was to the Second World War what the O4 was to the First World War – a standard locomotive type chosen by the government for mass production and use in military service overseas. Uniquely, both types are represented on today's GCR.

Restored to running order, it debuted on February 25, 1995 during the winter gala. A hugely popular and versatile performer, No. 48305 also visited several other heritage lines, including the GCR(N) in 2000. That June, it went to the Churnet Valley Railway to begin a five-year loan period agreed by Roger.

However, boiler work was needed and it ended up at Pete Waterman's LNWR Works at Crewe for a 10-year overhaul, during which more boiler work was found necessary.

Roger then asked to bring his 8F back to Loughborough permanently. An agreement was reached, and the David Clarke Railway Trust provided funds to complete the boiler repairs after which No. 48305 returned to the GCR on April 13, 2006. It re-entered traffic that May, but was withdrawn for a full 10-year overhaul in late 2011.

A star attraction at the January 2013 steam gala was GWR 4-6-0 No. 6023 *King Edward II*, carrying the early British Railways' express passenger blue livery.

A decade ago, the Great Western Society had hoped to send No. 6023 for running-in tests on the GCR following its ground-breaking restoration from Barry scrapyard condition with cut driving wheels. Now the original wish of owners has come true.

The locomotive arrived from Didcot Railway Centre on September 6, 2012, and underwent repairs to its boiler at Loughborough shed.

After a public launch at Didcot, No. 6023 suffered serious boiler problems while running in at the Mid-Norfolk Railway in the summer of 2011. The problems led to the cancellation of No. 6023's eagerly awaited main line debut, but the leaking tubes were repaired before it arrived on the GCR, and all that needed to be tackled were the stays.

In spring 2013, special permission was obtained from No. 6023's owning group to rename it as No. 6015 *King Richard III*, in recognition of the recent successful archaeological dig, which found the remains of the former king of England, Richard III, under a car park in Leicester.

No. 6023 is seen dazzling the army of photographers poised at Kinchley Lane – arguably the most popular vantage point in the UK heritage railway portfolio – on January 26, 2013. ROBIN JONES

The sole-surviving British Railway Standard 5MT fitted with Caprotti valve gear is seen in action hauling the 'Irish Mail' on February 4, 2006, during the winter steam gala. No. 73129 emerged from Derby Works in August 1956 as one of 30 built fitted with Caprotti gear. Withdrawn in 1967, it was rescued from Barry scrapyard in 1972 and restored at the Midland Railway-Butterley. It steamed again on February 22, 2004. ROBIN JONES

Another guest at the 2010 Golden Oldies gala was one which was built a quarter of a century before the London Extension, LSWR Beattie 2-4-0 well tank No. 30585 from the Buckinghamshire Railway Centre. It is seen leaving Rothley on May 28. PHIL WATERFIELD

WEST COUNTRY LIGHT PACIFIC *BOSCASTLE*

Bulleid West Country light Pacific No. 34039 *Boscastle* was built in 1946 at the Southern Railway's works in Brighton as 21C139 and entered traffic on September 16 that year in Southern malachite green livery.

First based at Stewarts Lane shed, it hauled expresses from London Victoria station to the Kent coast resorts of Margate and Ramsgate and the ports of Folkestone and Dover, including the legendary 'Golden Arrow'.

Renumbered 34039 at Nationalisation, in November, it moved to Brighton shed, where it became the first West Country class locomotive to carry the new standard British Railways passenger green livery in August 1949.

In May 1951, *Boscastle* was chosen for trials on the Eastern Region. Based at Stratford shed it worked services from Liverpool Street to Cambridge, Norwich and Harwich, but it was not a great success because of crew unfamiliarity with Bulleids.

In November 1958, it was rebuilt at Eastleigh Works, its streamlined casing being removed and it re-entered traffic in January 1959, being reallocated to Bournemouth shed shortly afterwards.

From there, it worked two-hour express trains to Waterloo, including named trains the 'Bournemouth Belle', 'Royal Wessex' and 'Pines Express'. Indeed, on June 19, 1959, *Boscastle* became the first rebuilt West Country to run on the Somerset & Dorset.

In September 1962, *Boscastle* was transferred to Eastleigh shed, working semi-fast trains to Bournemouth and London and occasionally the heavy 'Ocean Liner Special' between Southampton and Waterloo. The trains ran in groups of three to five to coincide with the arrival of the liners at Southampton Docks.

On April 27, 1963, it headed one of several football specials from Hampshire to Birmingham, when Southampton were playing Manchester United at Villa Park in the FA Cup semi-final. It was serviced at Tyseley shed for the return trip.

After clocking up 745,000 miles in service, *Boscastle* was withdrawn in May, 1965. It reached Barry scrapyard that September.

James Tawse, a member of Main Line Steam Trust Ltd in its embryonic days, suggested buying a West Country for use on the preserved Great Central, and found that of all those at Barry, *Boscastle* was in the best condition.

In November 1972 he bought No. 34039, which duly arrived on the GCR two months later.

In 1986, James formed the Boscastle Locomotive Syndicate to widen the ownership and raise essential funds for restoration.

Finally, on November 7, 1992, *Boscastle* moved for the first time under its own power, and was launched into traffic the following year, becoming a hugely popular performer.

In 1994, it visited the Gloucestershire Warwickshire Railway, and two years later, visited the West Somerset Railway.

However, long-running firebox problems compounded with boiler tube leaks led to *Boscastle* being withdrawn from traffic in 2000 until a full overhaul could take place. Boscastle Locomotive Ltd was formed in 2005 to fund this second overhaul, which is still underway at the time of writing.

Visiting Southern Railway Merchant Navy Pacific No. 35005 *Canadian Pacific* at Swithland on December 30, 1990. BRIAN SHARPE

During the Spring Bank Holiday of May 28-31, 2010, around 4000 visitors turned out for one the most unusual gala events ever held on the GCR, or any preserved line for that matter. The Golden Oldies gala featured Victorian locomotives and rolling stock, some of which were replicas of types from the dawn of steam. It was believed to be the first time since the 1830s that Liverpool & Manchester Railway No. 9 *Planet* had passed Stephenson's *Rocket* with passenger trains.

The replicas, the first from the Museum of Science & Industry in Manchester and the second from the National Railway Museum, ran with matching coaches between Loughborough and Quorn & Woodhouse, but no further because of the limited water capacity.

The NRM's *Rocket* replica and matching coach are seen preparing to depart from Quorn & Woodhouse. BRIAN SHARPE

Also appearing at the 2010 Golden Oldies gala was Furness Railway 0-4-0 No. 20, built in 1863 and now the oldest working steam locomotive in Britain. It is seen departing from Loughborough Central on May 30. BRIAN SHARPE

Malachite green double: Visiting Southern Railway Schools 4-4-0 No. 925 *Cheltenham* doubleheads with home-based N15 No. 777 *Sir Lamiel*. Both engines are part of the National Collection. HUGH BALLANTYNE

Visiting Jubilee 4-6-0 No. 5690 *Leander* storms through Quorn & Woodhouse with a TPO drop during the autumn 2008 steam gala. As LMS No. 5690, it was built at Crewe in March 1936 and named *Leander* after *HMS Leander*. Withdrawn in 1964, it was rescued from Barry scrapyard in 1972 for restoration at Dinting. Later sold to the late Morecambe GP Dr Peter Beet, it is still owned today by the Beet family and operated by the West Coast Railway Company from its Carnforth base.
DUNCAN HARRIS*

WITHERSLACK HALL: A GC VETERAN

It may have a thorough Great Western pedigree, but Frederick Hawksworth Modified Hall No. 6990 *Witherslack Hall* is a true veteran of the London Extension.

Built at Swindon shortly after Nationalisation in 1948, *Witherslack Hall* was selected to take part in the Locomotive Exchanges that year. The newly formed British Railways wanted to trial engines from different 'Big Four' companies on new territory to see how they fared outside the routes for which they were built.

Clearance issues meant the only non-Great Western route over which the engine could run was the Great Central main line from Manchester to Marylebone, over which it performed well. It also ran on tests between Plymouth and Bristol.

Halls regularly ran over the GC via the Banbury branch from Culworth Junction, and often reached as far north as Nottingham.

For most of its working life, No. 6990 was based at Old Oak Common, and was a regular performer on Paddington to Worcester services. In its final two years it was shedded at Bristol and worked cross-country services to South Wales, Weymouth and Salisbury.

No. 6990 was withdrawn on December 17, 1965, and arrived at Barry the following February.

Bought by the Witherslack Hall Locomotive Society, it arrived at the GCR on November 29, 1975. Its restoration took 11 years, and it finally entered traffic on August 30, 1986, being officially launched into traffic by railway artist David Weston.

Withdrawn for boiler repairs in January 1992, it returned to traffic four years later. Further boiler problems led to its withdrawal in 2001, when it went to Tyseley Locomotive Works for a 10-year overhaul, to be completed as funds permitted.

In January 2006, the David Clarke Railway Trust took over the ownership of No. 6990, which returned to the GCR two months later continue its overhaul. In October 2013 the boiler returned to Tyseley for the completion of repairs.

No. 6990's incorrect Collett tender has been exchanged with the Hawksworth tender from Severn Valley flagship GWR 4-6-0 No. 4930 *Hagley Hall*.

'JINTY' NO. 47406

One of the smallest members of the GCR fleet, but no less popular for it, is LMS Fowler 'Jinty' 0-6-0T No. 47406.

Built by Vulcan Foundry in 1926, it was initially allocated to Warrington and then Crewe South before spending 32 years at Carnforth.

BR Standard 9F 2-10-0 No. 92212 is seen departing from Rothley in late December 2000.

Built at Swindon in September 1959, it sheds included Banbury, Bath Green Park, Ebbw Junction, Tyseley and Carnforth, from where it was withdrawn in January 1968. It arrived at Barry scrapyard in September 1968, and left 11 years later after being bought by 92212 Holdings Ltd, which moved it to Loughborough in September 1979. Its restoration was completed in September 1996. It later moved to the Mid Hants Railway, where it underwent a major overhaul. It was bought by multi-millionaire enthusiast and locomotive owner Jeremy Hosking, and returned to service on the Watercress Line on September 11, 2009. It has also been hired for long periods to the Bluebell Railway in recent times. ROBIN JONES

Roger Hibbert's LMS 'Jinty' 0-6-0T No. 47406 returned to steam on January 30, 2010, in time for the winter gala. It is seen with a morning arrival at Rothley that day. ROBIN JONES

Withdrawn from Edge Hill in 1967, it arrived at Barry scrapyard the following summer.

Bought by the Rowsley Locomotive Trust in 1983, owner Roger Hibbert moved it to Loughborough six years later.

Restoration was completed in early 2010.

THE ORANGE ONE

Arguably the most striking locomotive at the Great Central Railway is a diesel, one of those built as part of the Pilot Scheme ordered by British Railways to replace steam traction.

Furthermore, it has a thorough Loughborough pedigree.

Brush A1A-A1A Type 2s, later Class 31s, were built by Brush Traction in the town, and entered service in November 1957.

In January 1960, D5579 emerged from the Brush Falcon Works in an experimental golden-ochre livery and was the only member of the 263-strong class built between 1957-62 to carry it. Sadly, it no longer survives.

Sister D5830 entered traffic on January 11,

1962 at Darnall, (Sheffield), and later received the TOPS number 31297. D5830 was one of the 68 class members to be fitted with electric train heating generators in the Seventies and was renumbered 31463.

Withdrawn in June 1996 with weak springs, the Type One Locomotive Company purchased it as a source of spares for No. 31418, and it arrived at the GCR on January 30, 1998 for dismantling. However, it was found to be in a better state than No. 31148, which was sold on. So, it was decided to return the 'spares' donor to running order, and it entered GCR service on April 23, 1999.

It did so in the golden-ochre livery carried by D5579, whose identity it adopted for a brief spell before reverting to the correct D5830.

It had been planned to run it in golden ochre for only a year before repainting it into an authentic livery for the locomotive, but it proved so popular with visitors that it has been retained.

Above: LNER K4 2-6-0 No. 61994 *The Great Marquess* departs from Quorn & Woodhouse with the 1.15pm dining service to Leicester on October 17, 2010, the train being formed of the superb Great Central first-class Pullman stock. Today's GCR, like the original, is famous for its dining services over the London Extension: the 'South Yorkshireman' is now the Saturday luncheon train and the 'Elizabethan' runs on Sundays, apart from special event days. Trains normally pause on Swithland Viaduct with its magnificent views across the reservoir to Charnwood Forest, while diners enjoy their four-course lunches. It was the only one of the six K4s that survived into preservation, thanks to the late Viscount Garnock who bought *The Great Marquess* from British Railways and overhauled it to working order. PHIL SANGWELL*/GCR

Class 45 D123 *Leicestershire and Derbyshire Yeomanry* approaching Kinchley Lane with the 'windcutter' rake on January 27, 2007 during the winter steam gala. ROBIN JONES

THE CLASS 45 PEAKS

British Railways' 126 express passenger Class 45 1Co-Co1s, as they became known, were built between 1960-62 at Crewe and Derby.

Several were named after British Army regiments using names formerly carried by the LMS Royal Scot steam locomotives. The class became known as Peaks as they were similar to the Class 44s, which had been named after mountain tops.

Two are present on the GCR. D123 was built at Crewe and entered traffic at Derby on October 28, 1961, hauling express trains on the Midland Main Line and also working cross-country routes.

Displaced by High Speed Trains, it ended its BR service days on trans-Pennine services from Newcastle and Scarborough to Liverpool and North Wales.

In April 1974, after being fitted with electric train heating, it became part of the 45/1 sub class and was renumbered 45125.

Also shedded at Toton, it was withdrawn from Sheffield Tinsley on May 7, 1987 and placed into storage at March.

The Railway Technical Centre at Derby used it as a dead load vehicle for testing the new Class 60 locomotives on its Mickleover test track during 1989-90.

Bought in 1991 by the Humberside Locomotive Preservation Group, which later became the Loughborough-based 5305 Locomotive Association, it was moved to Hull Dairycoates in March 1992 where major restored began. Another move followed, to Hull Botanic Gardens depot two years later, and in April 1998 it was taken to the GCR, where bodywork repairs continued.

Repainted into BR green livery, on June 22, 2000 at Loughborough Central it was named *Leicestershire and Derbyshire Yeomanry* by Lt Col Ridley Thomson and commissioned into

Making a rare visit from its North Yorkshire Moors Railway base for the GCR's Swithland sidings gala on May 10-11, 2014 was Lambton, Hetton & Joicey Colliery Kitson 0-6-2T No. 29, which was preserved in 1970. Its latest overhaul was completed in 2013. ROBIN JONES

traffic. The name was originally carried by Class 46 D163/46026.

No. 45041 was built at Crewe and entered traffic on June 25, 1962. It was named *Royal Tank Regiment* on September 24, 1964.

By the Eighties, it was mainly used on freight, so was not fitted with electric train heating apparatus for passenger work. On June 8, 1988, it was withdrawn from Thornby after sustaining a traction motor problem while working a stone train from Peak Forest to Leeds.

It was preserved by Pete Waterman and in 1994 taken to Crewe Heritage Centre.

He sold it on to the Peak Locomotive Company in February 1996 and restoration work began at the Midland Railway-Butterley.

When No. 45041 arrived at the GCR midway through 2012 it suffered from oil pressure problems, which were rectified by autumn the following year.

The presence of the pair along with a variety of other diesels goes a long way to fulfilling the GCR's mission statement of replicating a trunk route of the Sixties changeover years, with diesels running alongside steam.

With the excellent Ellis's Tea Rooms to the right, LMS Fairburn 2-6-4T No. 42085 is pictured at Rothley on June 22, 2008, while making an extremely rare visit away from its Lakeside & Haverthwaite Railway home. ROBIN JONES

Class 47 D1705 *Sparrowhawk*, one of five examples that briefly became Class 48s. NOTTSEXMINER*

LMS Jubilee 4-6-0 No. 5690 *Leander* heads 'The Waverley' from Loughborough Central during the 2008 autumn steam gala. BRIAN SHARPE

Visiting from the Swanage Railway, Bulleid Battle of Britain Pacific No. 34070 *Manston* departs from Loughborough Central during the October 2013 autumn steam gala. ALAN WEAVER

Class 31 D5830 carrying the experimental golden ochre livery worn by its scrapped sister D5579. ROBIN JONES

THE SPARROWHAWK THAT NEVER FLEW HOME

Another Loughborough product, Class 47 Brush Type 4 D1705 was built in the town's works in 1965 and entered traffic that November.

One of five locomotives to be built with a Vee Sulzer type 12LVA24 engine, it was also equipped from new with a Spanner Mk. III steam heat boiler. The generator was different from the ones in the 'normal' Class 47s as the engine rotated clockwise instead of anti-clockwise.

Allocated to Tinsley, it also ran out of Shirebook, Norwich and Stratford depots. Back at Tinsley by 1970, it was unofficially named *Sparrowhawk*.

It was converted to a standard Class 47, with a Sulzer type 12LDA28C engine in April 1971: before this, under TOPS it was designated as a Class 48. It was renumbered 47117.

It was the last Class 47 to provide steam

heat, and still has its complete Spanner boiler, although this is currently unserviceable.

Withdrawn with electrical faults in 1991, it was bought by Pete Waterman in 1993. He looked at the possibility of reinstalling a VEE engine and converting it back to Class 48.

It entered traffic on the East Lancashire Railway following repairs.

D1705 visited the GCR for a 1996 gala, during which it was offered for sale. The Type One Locomotive Company bought it from Pete, not having to pay transport costs as it was already at Loughborough.

Its BR blue livery was changed to the earlier two-tone green, and for an episode of the BBC drama Casualty, it carried yellow front-end warning panels for a time.

Now in 1960s green with the small yellow panel, it was officially named *Sparrowhawk* by Pete himself, at Loughborough Central on June 19, 2004.

One of the guests at the Swithland sidings gala in late May was GWR pannier tank No. 5786, which is now based on the south Devon Railway and has been reliveried into the London Transport livery which it carried between 1958 and 1969, when it was sold out of service to the Worcester Locomotive Society. As L92 is hauled freight and permanent way trains on the Underground, and therefore has a connection with the southern extremity of the London Extension. STEWART JONES

Steam returned to the Mountsorrel branch on November 23, 2013, when LMS 'Jinty' 0-6-0T No. 47406 ventured up to the railhead. STEVE CRAMP

The Mountsorrel branch reborn

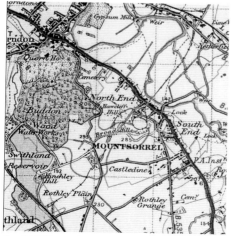

A mid-20th century Ordnance Survey one inch to the mile map showing the Mountsorrel branch leading from Swithland sidings to the granite quarry.

In the steam era, and for many years afterwards, thousands of industrial complexes all over Britain were linked to main line railways by private sidings, branch lines or sprawling internal rail systems.

The bigger concerns often had their own fleet of locomotives and stock, either for internal use, or more likely, for transhipment of goods and raw materials to and from the main line.

While Britain's heritage railway sector includes several classic industrial lines that were never officially part of the national network, the recreation of interchange facilities with the national network is comparatively rare. The Ribble Steam Railway carries bitumen traffic to Preston Docks, and in the early decades of volunteer operation, the Middleton Railway ran regular freight.

Before the Great Central Railway's London Extension was built, an industrial railway was built to convey stone from the granite quarries at Mountsorrel between Loughborough and Leicester to the Midland Railway main line near Barrow-on-Soar. Its first section opened in 1860.

A Class 37 would never have visited the branch in its operational days! Ballast laying is seen in progress in 2012. MALCOLM LAW

The Mountsorrel project has attracted volunteers who are not normally railway enthusiasts, of all ages and both sexes. MALCOLM LAW

In 1896, the line was extended south-westwards to Swithland to carry the ballast needed for the construction of the new Great Central main line.

Once the Great Central opened, what became known as the Mountsorrel Railway linked the two Leicester-Loughborough main lines. An extensive network of sidings was laid at Swithland where granite wagons were marshalled into trains which were sent on to their destinations all over the country.

However, the western section to Swithland Sidings gradually fell out of use in the 1950s and was mostly lifted in 1959. The quarry remained open, however, and the section to Barrow was replaced by a conveyor belt system in 1976, carrying stone to a network of sidings next to the main line at Barrow, which remain in use today.

Nature slowly but surely reclaimed the section from the quarry to Swithland.

In 2005, Railway Vehicle Preservations announced plans to relay three quarters of a mile of the branch to lead to a shed in which the group would store its priceless collection of historic vehicles, and secured a lease on the trackbed. However, the project stalled due to difficulty in obtaining planning permission because of environmental concerns.

Around this time, local resident Steve Cramp was researching the history of the Mountsorrel locality, where he had bought a house, and was astonished at the size of the extensive rail network in the locality. He was inspired to write a feature on the subject for the village magazine.

He dreamed up a small-scale scheme to re-create part of the branch, and three wooden plank open wagons were restored in the livery of the Mountsorrel Granite Company, complete with lettering. One of them was replicated in OO scale as a limited edition run of 500 models for *Heritage Railway* magazine.

When the carriage shed scheme floundered, Steve suggested restoring the branch itself. The idea of reinstating the branch as an added attraction to the main railway had also been mooted in a 10-year plan drawn up by former

Great Central chairman John East.

While many heritage lines have started off with industrial locomotive types and 'evolved' to restoring and running former main line steam locomotives to add authenticity, here is a scenario where locomotives which in the steam age would never be seen in operation on the national network could authentically interact with it.

The project's aim to re-create branch line trains is likely to see industrial locomotive types running a double track trunk railway where main line locomotives are the order of the day. Nowhere else is this regularly replicated in the preservation portfolio.

A UNIQUE COMMUNITY AFFAIR

It has always been an aim of the Mountsorrel project to restore the branch line corridor back to how it would have been during the original life of the railway.

It was recognised from the very early days of the project that the derelict and neglected route offered a wealth of potential, with changing landscapes and surroundings throughout its relatively short length of 1.2 miles.

The first steps taken were by six volunteers who cleared away the vegetation, after which many local people offered their services. Families got involved not because they were railway enthusiasts but because of their

In 2010, local artist John Cramp produced a limited edition watercolour of the Mountsorrel branch. The painting, The Way Forward, shows sole surviving Mountsorrel Railway steam locomotive, Peckett 0-4-0ST *Elizabeth*, leaving the Wood Lane bridge with a rake of Mountsorrel granite wagons. *Elizabeth* (works number 1759 of 1928) is currently based at the Rutland Railway Museum, where it is being restored. It is a long-term ambition of the project team to return this locomotive to the railway.

The Mountsorrel project team's volunteers have recreated three different types of the wagons used on the original line by the quarry company. They are seen parked at Loughborough station. ROBIN JONES

Fitting a check rail on one of the tight radius curves. MALCOLM LAW

Re-laying the quarry branch has continued in all weathers. MALCOLM LAW

interest in the village and its history.

Success has been achieved with the support of the local community, by working with schools and other groups, and by promoting ecological aspects of the project. There is now a core of approximately 120 regular volunteers offering different skills and time commitments to the project.

Local schools were involved with ecology study sessions as the route was cleared prior to reconstruction. These included the replanting of native wild flowers, the provision of bird boxes and the encouragement of other wildlife habitats. The project ran a series of visits that allowed more than 400 children to learn about their local history and also helped to boost the ecosystem along the sides of the track-bed. Children grew native wild flowers which they then planted alongside the route. The improved diversity of flora and fauna helped the ecology of the trackbed to return to how it would have been during the original operating life of the railway and has boosted the ecosystem generally.

This ecological emphasis allows the project to appeal to a much wider audience than it would have otherwise done. The junior ecology sessions gave very young children and their parents the opportunity to share an activity, recognising that involvement at this stage could well lead to general volunteering with the project in years to come.

In 2012, Mountsorrel Railway Wildlife Warriors, an ecology group for three- to 11-year-olds, was established. Children come along with an adult on periodic Saturday afternoons to sessions with a different focus or topic; e.g. birds, mini beasts, trees, plants and hoghouses (hibernation homes for hedgehogs!). Other activities, such as a mini archaeological dig or dry-stone walling, have

The Mountsorrel quarry time office in the 1870s, with a fan of sidings in front. MOUNTSORREL PROJECT

also been included and feedback from parents is positive and invaluable. And, occasionally, the parents end up as project volunteers.

Meanwhile, hedgerows have been laid with the help of other project members. More than 1100 sapling trees and bushes were planted along the line in the first quarter of 2012. As well as helping the hedges to thicken and regenerate, the process has also opened up views from the branch. When the line reopens it should be possible to ride along the branch behind a steam engine and see other steam trains crossing the GCR viaduct over Swithland Reservoir, a quarter of a mile away. Again, this will make the Great Central Railway and the associated Mountsorrel branch unique in the heritage railway world.

THE TRAINS RETURN

In 2011, the first train on the branch since 1959 ran when top ballast was brought to the line and this was followed, a few months later, by the sight of the first steam locomotive on the restored section of the branch.

The first revenue-earning train on the Mountsorrel Branch was a dining train for volunteers on November 23, 2013. Public services are expected to commence in mid-2015.

A number of Leicestershire employers have been helping the Mountsorrel Railway Project by encouraging their staff to volunteer in the community. Aggregate Industries, which operates Bardon quarry at Coalville, has sent teams of up to 15 volunteers on three occasions since the summer of 2012. Caterpillar, which has a plant at Desford, sent 20 volunteers to the Mountsorrel Railway on four consecutive days in November 2012. While in 2014, AON also sent some of its staff to help with track realignment.

So delightfully typical of industrial backwater and byways branch lines, the newly-ballasted Mountsorrel line is seen in May 2014. ROBIN JONES

As the project progressed, volunteers agreed a shared vision for creating a nature trail through the wood just south of the line. The volunteers' ideas involved a path, known as the Nunckley Trail, which would pass by as many as possible of the ecologically and historically interesting areas. The path makes its way to a picnic and viewing area where visitors will be able to watch the trains go by. It then passes wood carvings (made by another of our volunteers) back up to the entrance at Wood Lane.

The route is lined with logs down either side and in-filled with wood chippings to give a pleasant and clean surface to walk on. The trail has been widened for access and our younger volunteers assisted with dropping wood chippings along the path.

The route takes in several open areas that will be used for future Wildlife Warrior ecology sessions. In total the path is about one kilometre long, so makes a very pleasant walk and supporting attraction to the railway. Group members have created several areas for benches, which look out over both the railway and Nunckley Hill. The intention is to furnish the entire path with professional information boards to assist visitors with what they are seeing and this signage is currently being progressed.

The first revenue-earning train on the Mountsorrel Branch was a dining train for volunteers on November 23, 2013. STEVE CRAMP

The surviving quarry time office which is proposed for the new community heritage centre.
MALCOLM LAW

An artist's impression of the proposed heritage centre comprising the old barn (left) and time office (right). MALCOLM LAW

THE FIRST STATION ON THE REBUILT QUARRY BRANCH

There are currently two main developments underway.

Firstly, prior to the opening of the railway, a station platform is being built at Bond Lane, Mountsorrel.

A turning area for tractor-trailer rides from the nearby Stonehurst Farm and Motor Museum has been included in the plan in order to coordinate with another significant local tourist attraction. Limited car parking, mainly for disabled visitors, is also being provided. Despite the inherent access difficulties from the proposed platform being located in a cutting, it will be wheelchair accessible. Planning permission for the platform has been granted and in September 2014 work was in progress.

Secondly, and even more ambitiously, the Mountsorrel Railway Project has begun the process of creating a heritage centre, designed to tell the story of both Mountsorrel's and Rothley's village history.

At a later stage, there will also be a museum building linked by rail to the Mountsorrel Railway. The museum will house historical railway vehicles that once worked at Mountsorrel. A small platform will allow passengers to join and leave the railway and to visit the new attraction. There will be a tearoom, adjacent to the heritage centre.

The various components of the heritage centre will all be constructed in and around the disused Nunckley Hill quarry, which is situated close to Swithland Lane on the Rothley/Mountsorrel parish boundary.

Although the heritage centre will be partly 'new build', this will only be to unify elements of much older buildings that will be incorporated into the fabric of the new structure. Our hope is to re-site two historic granite buildings to Nunckley Hill, Rothley.

The first of these is a 200-year-old barn that stands nearby. This is due to disappear under

A view of the Charwood countryside as seen from the branch.
MALCOLM LAW

The foundations for the platform of Mountsorrel's first station as seen in September 2014. MALCOLM LAW

an over burden mound at the time of the planned expansion of the local quarry by its current operator, Lafarge-Tarmac. The barn will be rebuilt stone by stone and will be divided into two floors with the lower floor forming a Rothley heritage centre and the upper floor a Mountsorrel heritage centre. The barn itself has a colourful history having been used as a mess hall by German POWs working on the dam of the nearby Swithland Reservoir during the First World War.

The second building to be relocated is the old quarry time-office. This is the only surviving building from the original quarry yard and is, sadly, now derelict and in danger of being lost completely. The building will be moved and restored to retain its external appearance, together with the last remnants of an existing granite building, already on site, that is believed to have been the explosives' store.

The aim is for the heritage centre to cover all aspects of the history of Mountsorrel and Rothley, not just the railway and the quarry. Both villages have a wealth of history and the project hopes to be able to present that history on a permanent basis for visitors to experience. Mountsorrel is a 'working-class' village with not only the largest granite quarry in Europe but connections with other major employers such as Rolls-Royce.

By contrast, Rothley has a flamboyant past with direct connections to both the Knights Templar and the 19th century slavery abolition movement. Mountsorrel Heritage Group is working closely with the project with regard to the Mountsorrel Room in the heritage centre and similar contacts exist with both the Rothley History Society and the Rothley Heritage Trust to develop the other room in the centre.

It is fully intended that both the heritage centre and the railway itself will be as accessible as possible. Disabled passengers will be encouraged to use the parking spaces provided at either the proposed heritage centre or, alternatively, at the proposed station platform at Mountsorrel. The heritage centre site will be fully accessible, not only for those who are wheelchair bound, but also for those with sight, hearing, learning and other physical difficulties.

In addition to this the heritage centre will have a 'quiet room' which will be fitted out for use specifically for visitors who have serious illnesses such as cancer, cystic fibrosis, emphysema, etc. People with serious illnesses often find it difficult to have a day out because

Lineside hedge laying in progress. MALCOLM LAW

it can be over-tiring, or difficult to administer their medication. The project aims to provide a comfortable room where visitors with illness can go to rest and administer their medication. The project will not be providing medical facilities, just a pleasant and comfortable place where some visitors can go to take a few minutes away from the hustle and bustle before continuing their day out. This should help people in these situations to have more special time with their families.

It is intended that the enhancements to the railway and their maintenance will be self-financing through revenue from the tearoom and, consequently, visitors will be able to enjoy both the heritage centre and museum experience free of charge.

When completed, the Mountsorrel Railway will give another revenue stream to the Great Central Railway and will give economic support for other local tourist and visitor initiatives and the proposed local country park. On a wider scale, it will add an important new dimension to Britain's portfolio of heritage railways.

There has been extremely generous support from local companies and organisations, reinforced by support from local MPs and MEPs. In October 2014, planners gave the green light for the Mountsorrel and Rothley Community Heritage Centre, paving the way

for contractors to finish the work.

Costock Building Services completed the platform block work. The terminus will have a 190ft platform, with ramps at either end, sufficient for a locomotive and two coaches and a two-car diesel multiple unit.

Progress with the many developments on the Mountsorrel Railway can be followed at http://mountsorrelrailway.org.uk and anyone interested in becoming a project volunteer can contact project leader Steve Cramp at steve@mountsorrelrailway.org.uk

The old barn at Kinchley Lane which will become part of the new heritage centre.
MALCOLM LAW

CHAPTER 17

Trams are back

The Great Central Railway bridge is long gone, so modern trams have to cross the River Trent on tracks laid over the nearby Wilford Toll Bridge, before turning sharply east to pick up the old main line formation. NET

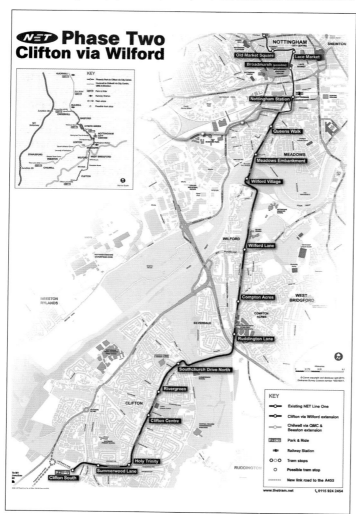

The route of the Nottingham Express Transit Phase 2 line to Clifton runs on much of the former GCR main line trackbed. NET

E arlier, we saw how the Great Central Railway built and operated its own electric tramway between Grimsby and Immingham Dock. It was closed by British Railways in 1961, but in 2015 a new tramway route was set to open on no less than the route of the GCR main line south of the former Nottingham Victoria station.

The new line is part of Nottingham Express Transit, a light rail metro system which was dreamed up in the 1980s.

The first section, Line One, was built by Carillion and opened to the public on March 9, 2004, having cost £200 million. It runs from Nottingham station on the Midland Main Line through the city centre to Phoenix Park and Hucknall, a total distance of 7¾ miles, of which 2½ miles are on street level.

It takes less than 30 minutes to ride from Hucknall into the city centre and just 20 minutes from Phoenix Park, and there are park-and-ride facilities at several stations. Reliability has been recorded at 99%.

Trams run every five minutes during peak times, and every six minutes during the weekday daytime, alternating between Hucknall and Phoenix Park, dropping to every 10 minutes Monday to Saturday evening and every 15 minutes Sunday evening. The trams run on 750v DC and have a top speed of 50mph. They are 100% low-floor vehicles articulated in five sections, and are 105ft long.

Unlike several other modern light rail city tram systems which struggled to carry the number of passengers originally predicated, Nottingham Express Transit was a soaraway success. By 2005, it was carrying 9.7 million people, far more than anyone had predicted, and made the case for further lines to be laid.

Construction and initial operation of Line One created 1000 new local jobs, and there has been an estimated 10% rise in residential property values along the route corridor – Hyson Green, Radford, and Hucknall – since it opened.

The current operator is Tramlink Nottingham, which was selected as the preferred bidder for the construction of Phase 2. The extension project was given the go-ahead by the Government on March 30, 2009, and funding was approved on July 31 that year. The scheme aims to reduce the number of car journeys into the city by four million a year.

This phase extends the system from Nottingham station to Toton and Clifton. Line 1 from Hucknall follows the same route to the station, and then continues to Toton Lane. Line 2 from Phoenix Park also follows its established route to the station, and then continues to Clifton.

It is this second extension that interests us here. For despite the fact that the bridge which once took the GCR over the River Trent and the viaducts and much of the embankment which carried it into Nottingham Victoria have long since been demolished, its route has been given a second lease of life.

The 5.4 mile Clifton tramline runs through densely populated residential areas to the south of the city, including The Meadows, Wilford/Ruddington Lane area and the Clifton Estate, to a new park and ride site serving the A453. It crosses the River Trent on the Wilford Toll Bridge, which, although widened, allows pedestrians and cyclists to continue to use it.

South of there, the tramline then uses part of the GCR formation including the surviving viaduct through Wilford and Compton. The old embankment has been partially rebuilt in places for the tram line.

The track continues along the disused embankment as far as the A52 Clifton Boulevard.

The full Line 2 service route from Phoenix Park to Clifton includes 28 tram stops.

The line to Toton will end near the site indicated as a hub for the proposed but controversial High Speed 2 line, on the section running from Birmingham to the north of England – in many ways a successor to Watkin's original vision for his GCR London Extension.

Both extensions are linked to the original tramlines by a bridge built across the top of Nottingham station.

The first powered test run involved a testing team from NET Phase Two construction contractor Taylor Woodrow Alstom taking Alstom Citadis tram No. 222 in the early hours of Friday, August 22, 2014, from Station Street via The Meadows to Wilford, before returning to Station Street. This initial run was for the purpose of gauging.

It became the first of the trams to cross the city's iconic new landmark, the 340ft Karlsruhe Friendship Bridge, which also includes two smaller adjoining bridges carrying tram tracks over Station Street and Queen's Road.

The new bridge attracted national headlines in 2013 when it was slid 500 yards from a nearby worksite and over the platform buildings and tracks at the city's Grade II listed station.

The bridge sits on the exact line of its GCR predecessor which was removed in the early 1980s. Two of the foundation caissons of the old bridge have been reused to provide part of the support to the new structure, although they have had to be strengthened with mini-piles.

Just like its predecessor, it will have two tracks.

Coun Graham Chapman, Deputy Leader at Nottingham City Council, said: "The bridge, which can easily be seen by commuters and visitors to Nottingham, is creating a new landmark representing the city's ambition and economic growth. It is a wonderful feat of engineering."

Up to 10 million people a year have used the NET system, and 90 million passenger trips have been made on the tram in the last decade. A further 10 million passengers a year are expected on Phase 2.

History is made as the first tram is taken over the Karlsruhe Friendship Bridge from Nottingham station on Friday, August 22, 2014. NET

Once the NET Phase 2 extension is complete, 20 of the 30 largest employers in Greater Nottingham will be within 850 yards of a tram stop, allowing staff to commute with ease and travel efficiently between employment sites.

Before the Phase 2 tramline routes were announced, there were those GC revivalists who looked longingly at maps of the vacant main line trackbed north of Ruddington and speculated as to how far it could be rebuilt into Nottingham – maybe up the south bank of the Trent. However, the tramway has now got there first.

What is now being talked about as a very long-term ambition is an interchange between the tramway and a relaid section of the heritage railway north of Ruddington. In theory, it would allow city residents and visitors to easily access the northernmost point of the modern-day GCR, and travel onwards behind steam trains or heritage diesels to Loughborough and Leicester North. In turn, heritage railway passengers could travel by tram into the city centre. On paper at least, it seems to be a win-win situation.

However, for the time being it must remain among the sackful of golden opportunities that await being opened once the new bridge spanning the Midland Main Line at Loughborough is built. Again, we all eagerly await that day. ∎

A model of the new bridge taking the tramlines across the top of Nottingham station. NET

CHAPTER 18

Loughborough relives the war years

LMS 'Black Five' 4-6-0 No. 45305, representative of a type that helped Britain win the Second World War. ROBIN JONES

A poppy drop takes place at the wartime event on June 9, 2013. GCR

QUORN & Woodhouse station was given its own part to play during the Second World War.

The War Ministry expanded the goods yard and added extra sidings, because it was considered that the countryside around here was reasonably safe from the attention of enemy bombers. Ammunition was stored in bases in the local area during the build up to D-Day.

The war years feel has never quite left the station, and each year it returns to the GCR with a vengeance for its phenomenally successful Wartime Weekend.

Platoons of re-enactors portraying Allied and Axis military personnel and British civilians descend on the railway, along with period military vehicles.

Each station plays a different role, with visitors able to travel between them to catch the action.

In recent years, Loughborough Central has become a British home front-themed station, where you can wave off the troops and bid a farewell to evacuees as steam trains depart.

Home Guard and ARP displays and drills are staged at a command post, and you may be lucky enough to glimpse Winston Churchill, George VI, Lord Louis Mountbatten or Field Marshal Bernard Law Montgomery.

Occasionally, three-mile guided walks of Loughborough showing where bombs fell during a Zeppelin air raid on January 31, 1916, are held.

King's Lynn, Great Yarmouth and Lowestoft were hit before the airship reached Loughborough. The first bomb fell in the yard of the Crown and Cushion pub, with another falling in The Rushes. More bombs fell in the streets, killing several residents. Shrapnel damage is still apparent on some houses.

During the Wartime Weekends, Quorn becomes a British, American and French station where soldiers, sailors and air crews from Britain, France and the US prepare for action. Often there is a flypast by vintage aircraft with a poppy drop.

A lone Luftwaffe bomber spots a potential ammunition train at Quorn & Woodhouse and dives in for the kill, with spectacular pyrotechnic results. ROBIN JONES

Musical entertainment rekindles the spirit of the roaring Forties. GCR

Wartime skirt hitch! PAUL BROWN/GCR

The driver of LMS Stanier 8F No. 8624 in conversation with an admiring passenger. GCR

Fond farewell. GCR

Taking to the skies. GCR

We'll meet again... GCR

The event features 1940s singers, and in 2014 a big band night made its debut. On occasions, hundreds of schoolchildren have been brought to the event to experience life as an evacuee.

As you cross Swithland reservoir, you leave Blighty behind and 'cross' the Channel into occupied territory. Keep your ID card at the ready!

Rothley is occupied by Germans in full kit, and you can even buy German beer.

Battle re-enactments are staged in the goods yard, and there are displays of Axis military vehicles.

Leicester North becomes Le Birstall, a French station, where the US army and French resistance attack the German garrison.

The new Greenacres restaurant there becomes a US army base. The event concludes on the Sunday at Quorn with a poppy drop, again from a vintage aeroplane, and church service to remember those who fell in conflict (Sunday only).

We shall fight them on the beaches... and over Swithland reservoir! ROBIN JONES

Is it one of ours? ROBIN JONES

Mock battle well under way at Rothley. ROBIN JONES

A German platoon lines up at Rothley. ROBIN JONES

The Yanks are here! ROBIN JONES

The spiv on board can get you anything you want – no ration book needed! ROBIN JONES

Fashions of yesteryear to the fore. GCR

Disembarkation time. ROBIN JONES

SNCF LE BIRSTALL

Leicester North takes on a new identity. ROBIN JONES

UNEXPLODED BOMB KEEP CLEAR

FILMING OF ENIGMA WITH MICK JAGGER ON THE QUORN & WOODHOUSE

June 5-8, 2000, saw Quorn & Woodhouse reprise its wartime role – when scenes for the movie Enigma starring Dougray Scott, Kate Winslet and Jeremy Northam, and co-produced and financed by Rolling Stone Mick Jagger, were filmed there.

The film was based on the Robert Harris novel about codebreakers based at Beaumanor Hall, a stately home within Woodhouse village.

The hall became a secret listening station where encrypted enemy Morse code signals were intercepted and sent to Station X at Bletchley Park by motorcycle for decoding. Beaumanor Park was the home of the War Office 'Y' Group for the duration of the war, and no doubt many top secret visitors arrived by the GC main line.

The film was due to star resident Bulleid West Country light Pacific No. 34049 *Boscastle*, which was built in 1946, the year after hostilities had ceased, but dirtied up to look like a LMS Royal Scot 4-6-0 from a distance.

However, Boscastle failed a boiler test. Needing another appropriate locomotive both for the film and scheduled services, West Coast Railway Company supremo David Smith agreed at short notice to send his LMS Stanier 8F No. 48151.

Thanks to a lightning response by haulage contractor Allelys, it was delivered to Loughborough within 48 hours.

However, the film producer decided that although the 8F was a locomotive built in huge batches for service at both home and abroad in the Second World War, Robinson O4 2-8-0 No. 63601 – a type which played a similar role in the First World War – was chosen instead.

Its number partially blacked out to 3601, and filmed from a distance, the 1911-built O4 became a mythical LMS wartime engine with a 1940s feel.

The O4 ended up hauling all of the trains in the film, an express passenger service, a freight working and a milk train with passenger coaches attached. One of the scenes involves a Nazi spy lying on the roof of a carriage to escape detection by police.

Graham Oliver, general manager at the time, said that Mick Jagger became aware of the GCR when his son played hockey at Loughborough Grammar School. "I was really impressed with Mick Jagger when we talked about the railway and he showed he was very knowledgeable about everything," he said.

"He has always been interested in the codebreaking and owns one of only three Enigma codebreaking machines known to exist. It was the double track that won the film contract for us, as the scenes require it."

Indeed, the presence of double track has secured several filming contracts for the line over the years.

Enigma, loosely based on actual events in March 1943, was released in 2001 to largely favourable critical reviews.

Mick Jagger inspects the GCR's rake of box vans during the filming of Enigma at Quorn & Woodhouse on June 7, 2000. LEICESTER MERCURY

CHAPTER 19

BRIDGE THAT GAP!
The greatest Great Central beckons

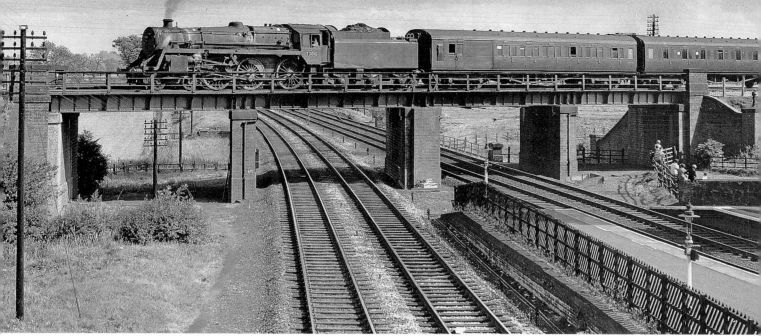

BR Standard 5MT 4-6-0 No. 73010 crosses the original Great Central bridge across the Midland Main Line in summer 1963.
T G HEPBURN/RAIL ARCHIVE STEPHENSON/GCR

For nearly three decades, one of the greatest dreams of the preservation movement has been to remove its biggest obstacle.

The Great Central heritage railways now occupy part of the London Extension between Nottingham and Leicester.

Divided by a gap of only 550 yards, each of them has much to offer.

As we have seen, the GCR between Loughbough and Leicester North has a record second to none in being able to replicate a trunk route from the Fifties and Sixties, with classic steam and diesel traction passing on the unique double track section.

Coming later in the day, the single-track Great Central Railway (Nottingham) has much to do to rebuild its intermediate stations and infrastructure to a similar standard. Yet it has the benefit of a main line connection, lacking on the line to the south, and there is more space around the railway, especially at Ruddington, for expansion and ancillary development if required.

Joining the pair together would be every enthusiast's marriage made in steam heaven. Yet there is the double problem of the missing bridge over the Midland Main Line at Loughborough and, worse still, the absence of the embankment and minor bridges leading up to it, both of which were removed in 1980, almost a decade before the early Great Central Railway (Nottingham) revivalists moved on to the Ruddington site.

Had both railways been at a more advanced stage, there is every likelihood that the bridge and approaches could have been saved, but it was not to be.

As the catch-up progress made on the GCR(N) intensified, thoughts inevitably and increasingly turned to replacing the bridge.

The long-held ambition of creating an inter-city heritage main line was the primary goal, but the southern GCR having access to the main line lagged not far behind. Look at the visiting charters that could arrive, boosting not only the line's visitor numbers but also the local economy.

Could big name main line steam locomotives be based at Loughborough? Could the GCR become a principal starting point for main line charters, ideal because of its position in the heart of England?

However, rebuilding the bridge perennially appeared as the ultimate will-o'-the-wisp. In the late Nineties, a figure of £3 million was bandied about, well out of the pocket of either and both

Members of the Network Rail team who inspected the site of the planned Great Central Railway bridge on November 8, 2013. DENNIS WILCOCK

Network Rail staff at the abutments of the bridge which carried the original Great Central Railway over Railway Terrace in Loughborough, on November 8, 2013. DENNIS WILCOCK

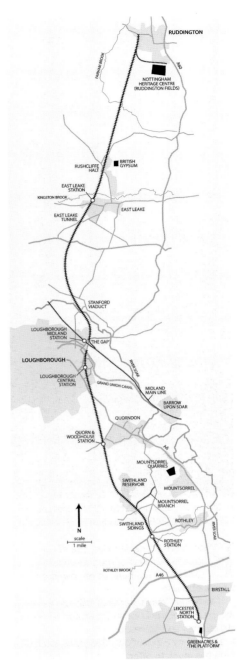

The 18 mile heritage trunk railway that will be created once the gap is bridged. GCR

lines. A decade later, £15 million was being talked about, in the same conversation as phrases like "it will never happen in my lifetime" or "it will never happen at all". Every time, the cost of the project remained out of grasp, even in the pre-recession years when at times it appeared that Britain was awash with grant aid.

All sorts of schemes were proposed to make it happen. One of the more prominent in recent times was rebuilding the Mountsorrel branch to carry granite trains from the quarry, which would then run over the GCR main line and the new bridge on to the GCR(N). The stone trains would then reverse down the spur and on to the Midland Main Line, the advantage being the replacement of the conveyor belt system that currently carries the stone to a point on the MML, and eradicating lorry movements.

The idea of the southern GCR building its own main line connection with a spur running from the north of Loughborough locomotive shed to the MML was vocalised, but that one quickly died a death.

Great Central Railway (Link) Limited, a separate company set up by the GCR to further the project, had held extensive negotiations with funding bodies behind the scenes for several years.

In April 2011, a £2.5 million bid for Regional Enterprise Fund grant aid to build the bridge was turned down, but upbeat GCR chairman Bill Ford said at the time: "We will be successful – there is no doubt about that."

However, the big breakthrough came with Network Rail's redevelopment of Reading station on the GWR main line.

A pair of bridge decks removed during the Reading project were donated to the GCR.

At first it was intended that the decks were to be used to replace a bridge on the GCR(N) across the public road crossed to the immediate north of Loughborough, but another possibility arose…

In June 2013, *Heritage Railway* magazine launched the exclusive story that everyone had longed to see in print: "Missing GC Loughborough bridge to be built by Network Rail."

On the day the magazine closed for press,

An early Network Rail visualisation of how the new bridge will look.

LNER A3 Pacific No. 4472 *Flying Scotsman* passing under the Great Central Railway bridge to the south of Loughborough Midland station on February 23, 1968, while heading for the Keighley & Worth Valley Railway. Soon, it may be seen running over it. DAVID MUGGLETON

its newsdesk heard that Network Rail had not only been officially engaged as contractor to build a new bridge linking the two heritage lines, but also an agreement had been signed.

The latest development came in conjunction with Network Rail's plans to electrify the Midland Main Line and presented a once-in-a-lifetime opportunity to reinstate the bridge at a far lower cost. It was too good to miss.

The GCR days later launched a £1 million appeal to rebuild the missing bridge by 2015.

There had previously been talk about having a double-track bridge in readiness for the time that a reconnected GCR(N) would lay a second line. However, the chance presented itself to have a bridge, albeit single track, by taking the two Reading bridge spans and laying them end-to-end with a central supporting pier.

Under the agreement, Network Rail would not itself provide any funding for the bridge, but would design it, prepare the application for planning permission and build it, working through its Derby office.

A smaller new bridge would need to be built over Railway Terrace in the industrial estate to the north of Loughborough, and the bridge over the Grand Union Canal will be refurbished.

Also, immediately south of the missing bridge, part of a factory car park now occupies the original formation. Discussions with the factory began to resolve the situation.

The bridge itself would cost a bargain £1 million and would be in place during 2015. The 330-yard southern embankment approach and ancillary works would cost around six and a half million at commercial rates, which may yet be reduced through further partnerships. If that took years to raise, at least the bridge, the biggest obstacle of all, would have been built in readiness.

THE PUBLIC IMAGINATION CAUGHT

The £1 million appeal raised £100,000 in its first fortnight, and was the fastest response to a fundraising drive in the history of the line.

GCR(N) publicity director Alan Kemp said: "We are humbled and flattered to reach one hundred thousand pounds so quickly. To be 10% of the way to the total in two weeks is incredible. Support has come from right across the heritage railway fraternity and beyond."

After years of pie-in-the-sky daydreams, there were visible stirrings on the ground. Network Rail surveyors were on site in July to

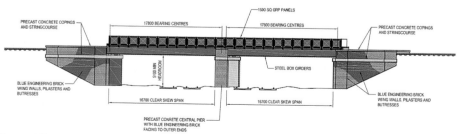

Plans of the gap dividing the Great Central Railway from the Great Central Railway (Nottingham). GCR

Bill Ford of the GCR and Alan Kemp of GCR(N) shake hands on one of the bridge decks on March 20, 2014. GCR

Right: Trial bores were carried out at the southern side of the missing bridge in a bid to ascertain the stability of the ground. GCR

continue design work, and again visited on November 8, a signal sighting exercise to ascertain what work might be required when the bridge is built.

Representatives from the boards of GCR plc and the GCR(N) began talks on the future structure of the completed 18-mile railway. A quarter of the target was reached on the 20th anniversary of the first public opening of the GCR(N)'s site at Ruddington.

By Christmas 2013, a third of the total was reached, boosted by a gift of £25,000 in memory of Loughborough shed volunteer and 9F Locomotive Charitable Trust trustee Peter Lang – who had worked on the restoration of No. 92214 prior to its first steaming at Butterley in 2003. A £15,000 grant was received from Leicestershire-based charity the Edith Murphy Foundation, which previously contributed to the restoration of the listed canopy at Loughborough Central.

In April 2014, the application for planning permission for the bridge was submitted.

The submitted plans detailed a two span steel box girder structure on brick piers and abutments, holly green in colour.

Two months later, the Bridging the Gap project was awarded a £1 million grant from the Government's Local Growth Deal, as part of an £80 million allocation to the Leicester and Leicestershire Local Enterprise Partnership. The money was allocated in two £500,000 segments, to make the rest of the project 'shovel ready'.

CHANGING DIRECTION

Around the same time, Charnwood Borough Council granted planning permission for the bridge.

That summer, experts offered to survey the Loughborough canal bridge on a sponsorship basis. XEIAD, a civil engineering consultancy specialising in difficult access, examined the disused bridge by providing two of its trained engineers for two days – work which would have otherwise cost the GCR tens of thousands of pounds.

Besides measuring and photographing the structure, they were also able to use a pontoon on the canal to examine the underside of the

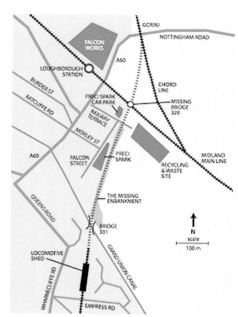

Contractors examining the Reading bridge decks ahead of the refurbishment work on March 20. Although they will not now form part of the bridge over the Midland Main Line, they will be used elsewhere on the GCR-GCR(N) link. GCR

Plans of the gap dividing the Great Central Railway from the Great Central Railway (Nottingham). GCR

bridge decks in detail. The report they produced was favourable, indicating that the structure is capable of being repaired.

Latest estimates place the Bridging the Gap scheme at £6.5 million.

UPGRADING THE BRIDGE

At the start of December, 2014, the GCR announced that not only had the bridge appeal passed the £700,000 mark, but also there had been a major rethink over how to build it.

No longer would the two second-hand Reading spans form the new crossing of the MML. Instead, a new design solution for the bridge has been agreed which will see an all-new 98ft bridge deck being built.

The move will eliminate the costs and risks involved with building a central pier, which would have originally been needed to support the salvaged decks, and will also reduce long term maintenance requirements.

Meanwhile the Reading decks will be used elsewhere in the reunification project speeding up the project and reducing costs.

In early 2015, dubbed The Year of the Bridge by the GCR, a contractors compound was established to facilitate the major construction work planned to start in the spring.

GCR managing director Bill Ford said: "These are truly exciting times for what we believe is one of the most high profile projects in national railway preservation."

A MAJOR DESTINATION FOR INTERNATIONAL VISITORS

Six months before the launch of the bridge appeal, another major announcement about a project designed to springboard the GCR on to the international tourist stage was announced.

In December 2012, it was announced that Leicester North had been earmarked as the site for a new multi-million-pound national-standard railway museum, one where trains would pull up alongside.

Plans for the new attraction were developed in partnership with both the National Railway Museum in York and Leicester City Council. It would feature locomotives, rolling stock and other artefacts from the National Collection – including LNER V2 No. 4771 *Green Arrow* and none other than GCR Director 4-4-0 No. 506 *Butler-Henderson*, which might well be coupled to Manchester, Sheffield & Lincolnshire Railway six-wheeler No. 946 which, as we saw earlier, is being restored at the Nottingham Transport Heritage Centre as a Quintinshill disaster memorial coach.

A series of exhibition halls and galleries would have direct access to the GCR's track,

Surveyors examine the parapets and decking of the Grand Union Canal bridge. GCR

The view from below: XEIAD surveyors examine the canal bridge at Loughborough from water level on July 9. GRAHAM WIGNALL

Computer graphic illustration of the new single-track bridge. GCR

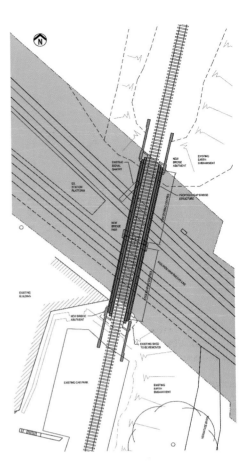

A December 2013 plan of the new bridge, drawn up before it was decided to have an all-new bridge deck without a central pillar. GCR

allowing engines and rolling stock to move in and out of the museum – and allowing visitors to get close to the exhibits and experience the day-to-day workings of a heritage railway, said a GCR spokesman.

A wooden carriage more than a century old will be restored in view of visitors, demonstrating the craft skills necessary to keep Britain's railway heritage alive.

NRM director Paul Kirkman said: "The prime objective of the National Railway Museum is to ensure that the National Collection is properly cared for and is accessible to the public. However, much of our collection is in store, out of sight of the public, or dispersed across various sites due to a lack of space.

"This new centre in Leicester, ideally situated in the heart of the country, would make it possible for us to share more of our historic artefacts with a much wider audience."

Leicester Mayor Peter Soulsby said: "The museum would house items which are of both national importance and local interest, complementing the nearby National Space Centre and Abbey Pumping Station and helping to enhance the city's reputation as an important visitor destination."

The museum could in effect become a third outlet for the NRM, which already has an outreach station in the Locomotion museum at Shildon.

A bid for £10 million in grant aid was submitted to the Heritage Lottery Fund.

However, in the spring of 2014, the Lottery turned down the bid – not because there was anything wrong with the project, but because it had run out of money.

However, the GCR was invited to apply again, and did so that November, facing a nail-biting wait until April to learn the result. If successful at the round one stage, the railway will at first receive a small grant which will allow the plans to be developed further. A successful second round application would see the full grant unlocked with the museum expected to be open around summer 2019.

Once the bridge is replaced, charter trains from all over Britain will be able to reach the new museum via the main line connection at Loughborough South Junction.

The impact on the local economy could be truly awesome.

Edward Watkin would certainly have approved.

RUNNING NORTH TO RUDDINGTON FIELDS

Once the bridge is built and the two heritage lines connected, inter-city steam trains will run from Leicester North to Ruddington Fields.

There is much to do on the GCR(N) to allow that to happen to a regular timetable.

Firstly extensive signalling work will have to take place on the GCR(N) and secondly there is the problem of accessing the spur to Nottingham Transport Heritage Centre.

Up to now, GCR(N) trains have to reverse south of the old Ruddington station, because the spur leaves the GC main line in a southerly direction.

That would be a major headache for lengthy GC inter-city trains, and so plans are in hand for a new south chord, so that they can run in and out of the northern terminus.

That will be the next big project once all else is completed. ∎

In early October 2014, contractors were on the site of the proposed new embankment, another key component of the reunification scheme, to carry out an environmental survey detailing the current state of the site and what effect rebuilding the embankment will have on wildlife and nearby water courses. These separate studies will inform the design work and ultimately a planning application for the construction of the rest of the link. GCR

CHAPTER 20

An alternative to HS2?

Long isolated from any operational railway, once-proud Leicester Central station survives in Great Central Way near the city centre, stripped of most fixtures and fittings. The booking office with ticket windows is intact and old timetables and signs are still on the wall, and the front taxi waiting area still stands and has its original lights and glass roof. The parcels office sign still stands above the door. The station buildings are now scheduled to be restored as part of the regeneration of the city's waterside area, with the arches made into shops. ROBIN JONES

Although it was allowed to downgrade to a secondary route during the Beeching era and then closed piecemeal, there are many who have since expressed doubts at the decision to axe the last trunk railway of the steam era, and others who have planned for it to be reopened.

In the Sixties, plans for a Channel Tunnel were being considered again, although no firm commitment was made, around the same time that the Nottingham to Marylebone line was in its death throes.

One of Dr Beeching's biggest success stories was in the carriage of freight. It was he who replaced the likes of the pick-up goods trains of old with the American-style container system which combined road and rail, and which became a global success as Freightliner.

John Edser, a member of Beeching's Central Planning Unit at British Railways headquarters in London at 222 Marylebone Road – ironically the former Hotel Great Central – wonders with hindsight if the London Extension should have been given a bigger role, if Freightliner had got off the ground earlier and the London extension lasted another three years.

As a backbone of England linking London (and therefore the Kent coast) to the major manufacturing towns of the north (running alongside the M1 at Lutterworth) and having less traffic than the other major routes, the Great Central may well have found itself in a prime position to become a key element in a new era of international freight transhipment.

A British-French government-backed scheme for a Channel Tunnel that started in 1974 was cancelled the following year, after the Labour Party returned to power.

In the late 1980s, Central Railway, a British company, proposed to build a new railway line with a generous loading gauge linking the Channel Tunnel with the north of England, using much of the old GC formation. The company claimed that it could significantly cut road congestion by carrying lorries on flatbed trucks.

The proposed Central Railway line would have run from Liverpool Docks to Sheffield using the disused Woodhead Tunnel and then turn south via the Erewash Valley, joining the former Great Central Main Line (much of whose trackbed is still intact) south of Leicester. At a rebuilt Ashendon Junction it would join the Chiltern Main Line, running alongside it on new tracks, then paralleling the M25 motorway, entering a new tunnel between Leatherhead and Merstham and then running alongside existing railways via Tonbridge to the Channel Tunnel terminal at Folkestone.

However, the £8 billion plans, which were backed by the French railway operator SNCF, were rejected by the British government in 1996 and again in 2003, mainly because of doubts over financing.

In January 2009 the Labour government established High Speed Two Limited, to examine the case for a new high-speed line and present a potential route between London and the West Midlands, possibly extending to the north and Scotland.

HS2 has been a huge source of controversy,

The Great Central Railway's Braunstone Gate Bridge was demolished in 2009 despite the efforts of conservationists to save it.

Arches on the western side of Leicester Central are now home to small businesses, with modern industrial units built on the trackbed above. ROBIN JONES

The proposed Phase 2 of the High Speed 2 line linking the West Midlands to the north of England. A station has been earmarked for Toton, where Line 2 of the Nottingham Express Transit will meet it, after running over part of the old GCR main line through Wilford. HS2

generating headlines like confetti. Business leaders have welcomed the prospect of a fast link to the capital, while environmentalists have opposed it in droves, and sceptics argue that the passenger fares would be so high that there would not be a mass public demand for it. Backers also said that Britain's trunk railway system is now bursting at the seams, and extra capacity is urgently needed.

In January 2012 the Secretary of State for Transport announced that HS2 would go ahead. It would comprise a Y-shaped network with stations at London, Birmingham, Leeds, Manchester, Sheffield and the East Midlands conveying up to 26,000 people each hour at speeds of up to 250mph. Phase 1 would be a 140-mile route from London to the West Midlands which would be constructed by 2026. Phase 2, from Birmingham to both Leeds and Manchester, would be constructed by 2033. Additional tunnelling and other measures to meet local communities' and environmental concerns were also announced.

While there has been cross-party support for HS2, there had also been similar opposition. However, a YouGov poll in September 2013 showed that only 29% of people in the Midlands (including Wales) supported the scheme, compared with 32% in the north and 34% in London. Many northern and Midland councils and MPs, who feared damage to their existing rail services, were strongly opposed.

GOING SOUTH?

However, all schemes to reopen the GCR route from London to the north have one thing is common – the section between Leicester and Nottingham which includes the two heritage lines would be bypassed, by diverting trains on to the Midland Main Line through Loughborough instead.

Such an approach is not taken out of love for railway heritage, but out of necessity. The pragmatic approach is that far too much of the old trackbed in Leicester and Nottingham has been lost to later development.

When modern-day GCR passengers arrive at Leicester North, on the far side of the A563 dual carriageway ring road, they spot the start of vacant trackbed on what appears to be an ideal route to extend back to Leicester Central. If only a bridge across that road could be built…

However, big as it would be, that would be only the start of the problems. In recent years, the railway had been involved in talks with the city council about a possible extension south of Leicester North station, to a new station one mile away, at Beaumont Leys Lane, close to the Abbey Pumping Station, National Space Centre and Abbey Park, and ultimately Leicester city centre. A run-around loop would be located at Beaumont Leys Lane, along with a single platform and station facilities a mile north of Leicester Central.

The heritage line's officials concluded that the restoration and rebuilding works would be too expensive and would not fit in with the council's timetable for the area. It was estimated that it would cost at least £6 million to go three quarters of a mile, with a replacement bridge over Thurcaston Road needed. However, south of Beaumont Leys Lane, many of the viaducts are now gone, and retail units have been built not only on the formation but inside Leicester Central station itself.

Nevertheless, many miracles have been performed in the heritage sector, and once the two Great Central railways are linked at Loughborough, who knows where the revivalists and the council might look in years to come, if vast amounts of external grant aid funding could be sourced.

Much of the through route has been lost, seemingly forever. To the south of Leicester Central lay Braunstone Gate Bridge, also known as the Bowstring Bridge, which took the GCR, and later a public footpath and cycleway, over Western Boulevard and the River Soar in Leicester.

The bridge had been in a poor state of repair following years of neglect by the local council which eventually demolished it in 2009 in the face of loud protests from Leicester Civic Society as well as many local people. On September 25, 2010, the society unveiled a memorial plaque to the former bridge on the facade of a nearby building

The chief executive of Central Railway was Alan Stevens who is no longer actively involved in promoting the Great Central scheme – but was this year elected as a UKIP county councillor in Great Missenden, along the HS2 route in Buckinghamshire.

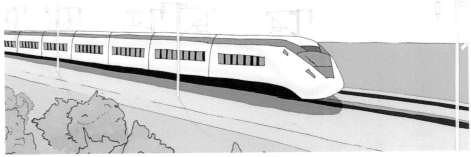
An artist's impression of what a 225mph HS2 train might look like. HS2

CHAPTER 21

The secret Great Central Railway

In addition to the sections of the original Great Central Railway that have been reopened as heritage lines, there is another length that has been built.

An operational, but strictly private, standard gauge heritage line has been laid at the remains of Finmere station in north-east Oxfordshire, where some of the platforms survive.

The site was acquired several years ago by a member of the Coulsdon Old Vehicle & Engineering Society, a private engineering club, which is based in south London.

Group member Gordon Laming explained that the original idea was to use the site for vintage road vehicles, but there was a subsequent change of direction and it was brought back into fully fledged rail use.

The running line was created from track that had been salvaged from the East London Line project.

Currently, the site is strictly out of bounds, and visitors are allowed on to it by invitation only. It is surrounded by a high steel fence, while neighbours and a local farm regularly keep watch on it.

Finmere station, which lies 54½ miles north of Marylebone, was opened along with the rest of the London Extension in March 1899.

The construction of the section through Finmere by Newcastle-upon-Tyne civil engineers Walter Scott & Co required major

Lonely Finmere station refused to give up on its railway past. ROBIN JONES

earthworks. To the north, a cutting of 180,000cu yd had to be excavated, while to the south the railway crossed an embankment the excavation of nearly 200,000cu yd. These earthworks reflected the Great Central's policy of eliminating level crossings on the London Extension, considering them to be a source of danger, inconvenience and cost.

As a result, bridges were built to prevent the need even for little-used crossings. A timber overbridge was built to the north of

Finmere for use by the local Grafton Hunt.

Finmere station was typical of the GCR standard style. It was reached via a flight of steps leading up from the centre of a road underbridge, each track having a separate bridge span.

A house was provided for the stationmaster and land set aside for the future provision of railway cottages. It had a small goods yard with a cattle pen, coal staithes and a goods store. The station was originally named

Class 73 electro diesel No. 73130 at Finmere, still fitted with additional coupling equipment for hauling Eurostar units. ROBIN JONES

Finmere for Buckingham, as opened in 1899.

The station buildings have long since gone, but some of Finmere's platforms survive. ROBIN JONES

Finmere for Buckingham, but as Buckingham lay miles away and was served directly by the LNWR's Buckingham station, it was hardly convenient to alight at Finmere in order to reach the historic county town. Indeed, Finmere village itself lay ¾ of a mile away.

Horse traps waited under the shelter of the road underbridge to ferry passengers to their destinations. Soon, a Paxton & Holiday livestock market appeared on land next to the station, while the building of the nearby Shelswell Inn began in May 1900.

In 1923, Stowe School opened a short distance across the nearby fields, with the station being used by staff and pupils.

Finmere station became a popular destination for daytrippers from London, with two or three special services running on Sundays. Once they had alighted, the passengers often found they faced a four-mile walk to Buckingham in the absence of local conveyances.

As more wealthy residents moved into the area, a slip coach service to Buckingham was introduced in 1923 for them to commute to London, Among them was LNER director Charles William Trotter who lived at Barton Hartshorn Manor. A slip coach on the 6.20pm from Marylebone reached Finmere at 19.28pm, the guard releasing the last carriage as the service approached the station. This carriage braked as it entered Finmere, which enabled expresses to continue without stopping.

After setting down at Finmere, slip coaches were worked forward to Woodford. The fastest service to Marylebone from Finmere in 1922 took one hour and nine minutes on an express, which stopped only at Aylesbury.

Finmere station had an extra lease of life during the Second World War because of its proximity to military camps and airfields. However, after 1945, its use declined in the face of competition from cars and buses, leaving the beginning and end of the school terms at Stowe the only busy periods.

In 1961, the British Transport Commission proposed closing the station, but Oxfordshire County Council and Finmere Parish Council objected. They were merely staving off the inevitable, as the station closed to passenger traffic in March 1963, with freight facilities lasting until October 5, 1964. Trains continued

to pass through until the London Extension was finally closed in September 1966.

Rails, however, are back at Finmere – even though they may yet be ripped up again, to make way for High Speed 2, a project announced several years after the society bought the site and moved in.

The venue has one item of motive power – Class 73/1 electro-diesel No. 73130. Also on site are several former Southern Region coaches, including two EPB sets, which have been repainted in green.

No. 73130 is occasionally used to haul at least one of the sets up and down the running line, lying in the station precincts.

The locomotive was outshopped by English Electric at Vulcan Foundry on July 13, 1966. It was renumbered from E6037 on New Years Eve 1973, and on July 2, 1988, it was named *City of Portsmouth*. The name was dropped in 1996.

It became one of two Class 73s owned by Eurostar, the other being No. 73130. They were specially modified with additional coupling equipment to enable them to haul a Eurostar unit. Based at North Pole depot, they were

used to rescue broken down Eurostar units.

When Eurostar moved its operations to the new Temple Mills depot and on to the overhead wiring of High Speed 1 – the Channel Tunnel Rail Link – in 2007, both became redundant.

No. 73118 was loaned to the Bar Rail Centre, while No. 73130 was moved to an abortive project to establish a railway staff training Railschool scheme on the closed North Woolwich branch.

Gordon Laming has said the owner would be applying for compensation if HS2 does indeed go through the site.

However, he added that if a different route for HS2 was ultimately selected, meaning Finmere's 21st century railway is allowed to remain, the site may be opened the public.

"If we were going to stay here, we could get permission to run south, maybe miles, as far as Twyford," he said.

That would be a stone's throw from Calvert, north of which a spur installed in 1940 links the surviving section of the GCR main line, which passes through Quainton Road to the Oxford-Bicester-Milton Keynes route.■

Restored Southern Region stock at Finmere today. ROBIN JONES

CHAPTER 22

The Coalfield Line

While the *Mardy Monster* was undergoing a boiler overhaul, another industrial locomotive with a mining pedigree was hired to cover for it. Former NCB Northumberland Area Vulcan Austerity 0-6-0ST No. 5309 Of 1945 was brought in for the 2014 season. JAMES HYMAS

The *Mardy Monster*, displayed at Railfest 2012 because of it being Britain's most powerful industrial steam locomotive. ROBIN JONES

Yorkshire Engine Company 0-6-0 diesel hydraulic No. 2895 of 1963 *Earl of Stafford* in action on the Elsecar Heritage Railway. BRIAN SHARPE

One final heritage line which was once part of the Great Central empire is the Elsecar Heritage Railway.

It occupies the upper part of the single track Elsecar branch of the South Yorkshire Railway. The branch ran from Mexborough to Elsecar via Cortonwood, crossing the Dearne and Dove Canal by lifting bridge, and opened for mineral traffic on March 1, 1850, linking to the main line to Barnsley at Elsecar Junction.

Serving Earl Fitzwilliam's colliery in Elsecar, the coal was forwarded to the GNR for shipment to Boston docks.

The Manchester, Sheffield & Lincolnshire Railway leased the SYR in 1861, having already allowed the company the use of Sheffield Victoria station. An Act of June 23, 1864, allowed the MSLR to take over the SYR for 999 years, and further powers were obtained in 1874 for a full takeover.

The line ran near the earl's Wentworth Woodhouse estate, and he ran private trains on the branch from his own covered station at Elsecar. Some of these trains from his Elsecar station went to Doncaster races, and he even operated trains for the Prince of Wales, later Edward VII, when he stayed at Wentworth Manor house.

The last part of the branch fell into disuse in 1984 when Cortonwood Colliery closed, the section to Elsecar having closed some years earlier.

The Miner's Strike of 1984-85 which pitted the National Union of Mineworkers led by Arthur Scargill against Margaret Thatcher's Conservative government began at Cortonwood Colliery. On March 5, 1984, miners at the colliery in Yorkshire and others walked out after being told it was to close.

The following day the unions were told that Cortonwood was just the first of a wide-ranging programme of closures that would shut 20 pits, leaving 20,000 miners out of work.

The Elsecar workshops were built in 1850 to facilitate a more effective management of the various industrial enterprises around the earl's estate. The National Coal Board took over the workshops in 1947 following the nationalisation of the pits. As the collieries began to close the demand for the workshop facilities began to decline, eventually leading to their closure.

In 1986 the Department of the Environment listed most of the buildings to be of special architectural or historic interest. Barnsley Council bought the workshops along with the Newcomen Beam Engine in 1988 and started a programme of conservation and restoration.

The council decided to reopen the workshops as a tourist attraction, the Elsecar Heritage Centre, in the early Nineties, with part of the branch relaid as a heritage railway. The first steam locomotive to arrive on site, Avonside 0-6-0ST No. 1917 of 1923 was named the *Earl Fitzwilliam* in memory of the former use of the line.

The first passenger trains ran in 1994, and on March 1, 2006, responsibility for the operation of the railway was transferred by the council to the Elsecar Railway Preservation Group, now Elsecar Heritage Railway.

No. 1917, which had hauled most of the passenger services since the opening, was withdrawn in 2002 when its boiler ticket expired, and is awaiting overhaul.

As of 2014, the standard gauge line runs for 1.25 miles between Elsecar to the present terminus at Hemingfield and features gradients as tough as 1-in-40.

Work is under way to relay the line back to the site of Cortonwood Colliery, giving a running length of 2½ miles. It is planned to build a new station called Cortonwood Colliery with a permanent exhibition outlining the story of South Yorkshire's coalfields and the mine's place in the strike. The railway has duly rebranded itself as the Coalfield Line.

On April 19, 2013, the railway completing the rebuilding of the Tingle Bridge Lane level crossing, which for officials was hitherto as insurmountable a barrier given their limited resources as the missing bridge at Loughborough is to the two GCRs. Once the crossing was in place, it paved the way for tracklaying to Cortonwood to start the following summer.

The current base of the railway is behind the Elsecar Heritage Centre. Here are located the railways engine sheds, workshops and offices. Elsecar station received a major upgrade including a new booking hall and station buffet during the winter of 2011/12.

The pride of the Elsecar locomotive fleet is the *Mardy Monster*.

Built in 1954 for Mardy Colliery, with a nominal tractive effort of 29,527lb, Peckett OQ 0-6-0ST No. 2150 is one of the most powerful industrial steam locomotives ever built in the UK, hence its nickname. Its power is equivalent to that of a LMS 7F, and in that respect, it might well not be out of place on today's Great Central Railway at Loughborough.

It moved to the Swanage Railway in 1979, but never ran there, and reached Elsecar after being sold in the early Nineties. It was a guest at the National Railway Museum's Railfest 2012 event at York and spruced up with a new coat of green paint. ■